MW00814664

REALISTIC
FLIPPING

A Beginner's Guide to
Renovating Homes for Profit

JIM CUNNINGHAM & **CRAIG WELCH**

Published by Take 42 LLC
1601 State Route 35 #432
Middletown, NJ 07748

www.realisticflipping.com

Cover and interior design by Take 42 LLC
Copyedited by Kathi Welch

Copyright 2006 by C & W Renovations LLC

All rights reserved. No part of this book may be reproduced in
any form or by any means without permission in writing from the
author, except for the inclusion of brief quotations in a review.

ISBN 0-9770698-1-8

Table of Contents

Introduction

So, you want to make money in real estate? Great idea. Even though most of the prognosticators tell us that the real estate boom is over, or at least almost over, we firmly believe that there is still a lot of money to be made for many years to come. You believe that too, or you would not have read this far! So read on... this program will help you safely become rich by buying, renovating and selling real estate.

But you're not going to get rich quickly, at least with our program. Oh, there are lots of programs out there that claim to be able to make you rich in days, weeks or months, all with "no money down." This is not one of those programs. Sure, "get rich quick" real estate programs will work if everything goes perfectly. But tell me, when was the last time that everything went perfectly in your life or business?

Our program shows you how to start carefully and build a business that will, in time, cause you to become rich. You will not be rich in a couple of months. But neither will you become broke or destroy your credit in a couple of months. Over the course of a few years you can expect to earn a substantial amount of money if you are prudent, work hard, and follow our program, even if you only work at it part-time. Fair enough?

Our methods are tried, tested, and sound. We did not set out to write a book, nor did we set out to become rich. We simply worked, researched and stumbled our way into a successful paradigm, had a lot of fun renovating homes, and made a bunch of money. And now it is our joy to share what we have learned with you.

chapter 1

The Genesis of a Dream

Have you noticed that folks are making money in every aspect of the real estate market? LOTS of money? We did. And moreover, our observation was that many of those folks making a lot of money were (and are) morons. Heck, how could we do worse than they? It just didn't seem possible to lose.

Well, we were wrong about that. It is possible to lose, and lose BIG. We'll spell that out in another chapter. But fortunately for us (and for you, benefiting from our experience) we were (and are) not morons and we were not trying to get rich in a day, a month, or even a year. We simply figured that we had the minimal skills and tolerance for risk that it would take to try out the whole "home flipping" phenomenon and make a few bucks.

Craig's day job includes consulting and an Internet business. Jim's day job is that of a pastor and regional director of a Christian youth organization. We are not professional contractors or real estate specialists. What we collectively brought to the table in terms of abilities was this.

- A love of adventure and a tolerance for risk

- Loving, supportive wives who were willing to trust us with our family assets

- A great friendship, high trust level in each other, and enjoyment of each other's company

- A shared ethic of honesty and integrity

- The belief that God would honor a hard day's work

- Flexible day-job schedules

- Some business savvy (mostly Craig)

- Some mechanical ability and experience with home improvement (mostly Jim)

- The ability to laugh at ourselves (and, on occasion, others)

- The desire to make a few dollars to help with college funding, vacations, and appreciating our wives

There you have it. You probably have more assets than that. It was hardly an impressive résumé, but it worked out wonderfully.

We found a realtor (much more on that later), and she found us a nightmare of a property with good potential in a nice part of a bad city. We worked really hard for two months, sold it in five days, and netted $50,000. We were stunned to make that much money. Our original projection was that we would net perhaps as much as $15,000, which was a ton of money in our eyes. We made mistakes, learned many valuable lessons, had our core values affirmed, enjoyed the work, and made more cash than we ever dreamed we could. And pretty soon we decided to incorporate and see if we could do it all over again. Almost to our surprise, we found that we could.

C & W Renovations LLC has averaged a net profit of over $40,000 on each low/mid range project we have undertaken. If you count high-end projects, the average profit climbs impressively. Do not count on replicating the results of our initial project on your first try. We don't bank on making that kind of money on every project, even with all of our experience! We are having fun, making money, and enjoying the ride. You can, too.

chapter **2**

Home Flipping
Defined

In this book we use the term "flipping" every so often. The American lexicon has not decided what "flipping" means yet. Some say flipping is the illegal buying and selling of homes while most define flipping as a quick renovation and resale. We actually like the term "flipping" because there needs to be a term to define what we do. Renovating is too often confused with what a contractor does to your home when you need a new kitchen.

Therefore we will use both terms in this book. Please note however that when we refer to "flipping" we are referring to a short-term renovation of a home that we intend to sell as soon as renovation is complete. When we talk about "illegal flipping" or "unethical flipping" we mean just that—illegal and unethical.

So it may be said that we "flip" homes, but more precisely, we renovate homes, and then sell them to make a profit. That's not unseemly, that's American! Seriously, there are folks out there who lack integrity and who are out only to turn a quick buck, no matter who they have to run over to do it. If you are one of these folks, don't read any farther. This book will be a waste of your time. In our program you're going to have to actually work for your profit!

What's the distinction between what we do and illegal or unethical flipping? It is fairly simple. Here are some of the basic differences:

Unethical Rehabbing/ Flipping	What We Do
Out for a quick profit by any means	Cognizant of the work involved and willing to do it
Valuation and appraisal schemes and scams	Honest research on the market, and honest valuation of the product
A fresh coat of paint covers a multitude of evils	A fresh coat of paint after the real work is done
Quality: "You can't see it from my house"	Quality: "Our reputation matters"
Are we benefiting our checkbook?	Are we benefiting the neighborhood?
Use people as means to an end	Develop relationships and you will get what you need from people who are glad to work with you
Money matters	Money matters, but so do relationships and integrity
Conspiracy among banks, appraisers and investors to deceive	Honest use of money and honest appraisal of the home

From the start, C & W Renovations LLC's core values included honesty and valuing people. We also value neighborhoods, and we desire to see everyone benefit from our work, not just us.

On the other hand, there are many people who are looking to make quick money in the real estate industry by any means, as long as they turn a profit. The industry is rife with schemes that are being used to leverage real estate into easy money. "Investors" may purchase dilapidated houses for a below market price and rally their teammates for the conspiracy. They recommend a mortgage broker who will help people get loans that should otherwise not get them. They will have a recommended appraiser that will look at the outside of the house (drive-by) and give a nice fat appraisal. They might also involve a bank in getting the buyer "help" with documents needed to be approved for a mortgage.

These investors do not care about the buyer, the neighborhood or the legality of their dealings. All they care about is a profit, which they are sure to make if they are smart enough. Although they may "win" in the end, everyone else loses in this game. Laws have been broken, a buyer now owns a property with a mortgage that he cannot pay, and his home is worth far less than he believes it is. If the owner defaults on his mortgage, the house is likely to become a vacant eyesore in the neighborhood once again. The investor has made a profit, but he and his cronies are the only ones who have gained. We find this kind of behavior short-sighted and reprehensible.

Some of these flipped properties are bought not by homeowners, but by "professional landlords" who are also out to make a quick buck. Think about it: there is a dilapidated house in your neighborhood. It may or not be occupied, but it is an eyesore in any case. It is an irritant, a detriment to your own property's value, and an embarrassment to you and your neighbors.

Someone comes along and buys it for a song, mows the knee-high grass, puts a fresh coat of paint on it, and sells it for a great price to an investor who can rent it for a profit. In the process, the investor makes $40,000 by doing almost nothing to this "distressed property" because he had it reappraised by a drive-by appraiser who has no idea of its real condition and is using your property value as a benchmark for the appraisal.

It is now rented by someone who has no pride of ownership, and probably could not care less about its condition. Who washes a rental car? So the house rapidly becomes an eyesore once again. Who's happy now? The investor is happy. He made $40,000 on your property's value and is laughing his way to the bank. And perhaps the absentee landlord is happy, too. He is collecting some rent and now has a fabulous tax break on his rental property, while avoiding putting any money back into the house for repairs and upkeep.

Who is unhappy? You and your neighbors, for starters. This house and its tenants are wreaking havoc on your property value. And the town authorities, who have to continue to deal with an unsafe home and an eyesore, are certainly not happy either.

But there are other scenarios where everyone wins, and these are the kinds of deals that we make. Here's an alternate scenario:

An investor buys that same property. He invests $30,000
fully renovating it and makes it one of the nicest homes in the
neighborhood. He strikes up a friendly relationship the neighbors
and lets them know that the house will be available soon for a fair
price. Perhaps the neighbors have friends or family looking for just
such a house! The home is safe, beautiful, and will increase the
property values in your neighborhood. It is ultimately sold to a nice
family who value their new home and your nice neighborhood.

Who's happy now? Well, the renovator is happy because he made
$35,000 in the course of doing an honest three months' work. The
buyer is happy because he just bought a beautifully renovated
home, one that he can take pride in for decades to come. And you
are happy because this home has increased your property value,
contributed to a safe and beautiful neighborhood, and provided
you with neighbors who you may soon call friends. The town
authorities are delighted as well. Everybody wins.

And the renovator made more than money—he made friends, built
a great reputation, and he can sleep at night, not worried that he
will face a lawsuit for shoddy repairs and workmanship. He built
a relationship with some good contractors, improved his credit
rating, and is in a great position to renovate another home in your
neighborhood.

Yes, you can make money simply turning homes over for a profit.
But we believe that there are some things that are even more
important than money. That is why we renovate and resell homes
ethically. And we think you will be happier in the long run if you
do, too.

chapter **3**

What Do You Need to be Successful at Real Estate Renovation?

The get-rich-quick schemers want you to believe that anyone can
make money in real estate. That is false. It does take a certain
number of assets. Not just time and money, but some important
intangibles as well. Here's a list of assets that we have found to be
imperative. We believe that if you lack these assets, your chances
of being successful diminish rapidly.

Courage!

To quote the cowardly lion in the Wizard of Oz, "What makes
the elephant charge his tusk in the misty mist or the dusky dusk?
Courage!" This is not a no-risk proposition. You are taking a risk.
You could lose money. Lots of money. Do we think that is likely?
No. But it is a possibility, directly proportional to your desire to cut
corners and avoid hard work.

One of the greatest assets we brought to the table as we began to
renovate homes was courage. We are risk takers. Craig likes to
kite-surf, rock climb, and drive really fast cars. Jim likes to ride
motorcycles, invest in antique cars, and scuba dive. And both of
us are willing to risk our families' money, within reason, to make
more money. Fortunately for us, our wives are, to a large degree,
indulgent of their husbands' risk taking, mostly because we have
accumulated enough of a track record to build trust in that area.

We believe that exercising courage is a good thing in and of itself.
Jesus told a story, a parable, of three servants who were entrusted
by their master with varying amounts of money and asked to invest
it. The one who took a risk and invested well was rewarded with
more, while the one who buried his cash in the ground for "safe

keeping" was admonished and what he had was taken away. One of our core values is that God gives us assets to invest and enjoy, not to bury in the ground.

It should be noted that we are *responsible* risk takers. We know the risks, take precautions, and are aware of and prepared for potential negative consequences. Some people are wild risk takers, and we certainly are not advocating anything like that. You can, and likely will, lose your shirt if you throw caution to the wind and believe everything you hear about real estate. But if you don't have the stomach to lay out $100,000 to $200,000 or more with no promise that the real estate market won't tank, you'd better re-evaluate home renovation as a career choice.

People Skills

Both of us have had many years of experience in dealing with people. Our "day jobs" require contact with many people on a regular basis. Our lives are full of fulfilling, mutually-beneficial relationships. We have both served in churches and on various boards and committees. We have been elected and selected by our peers at various times in our lives. We are friendly, outgoing, confident and likeable. People are drawn to us and we make friends easily. We also have an innate ability to understand people and be understood by them.

People skills have been more valuable to us than Craig's MBA or Jim's experience with a claw hammer. Renovating and reselling homes is not simply a business, it is a "people business." If you don't have good people skills you may be able to develop some by taking the Dale Carnegie course or some such seminar. Or, be sure to find a partner who will deal with the dozens of people you will encounter in every phase of this endeavor while you stay in the office and work on spreadsheets!

The Ability to Lead People

You will be working with all types of people: blue collar people, white collar people, nice people, mean people, honest people and dishonest people. And if you do not have the ability to figure out what kind of person you are dealing with and gain the upper hand in your negotiating, you will be at their mercy. And that means that they will be all too happy to make the money that you should be making.

When a contractor arrives on the site, he is immediately looking to establish an advantage. It may even be subconscious, but he is inevitably going to try to convince you of something that you either do not know or are unwilling to believe. He will tell you that you really need to pull of the entire roof, when what you had in mind after conferring with your home inspector was a simple replacement of the outer roofing material. Or he will tell you, "Nobody will renovate that kitchen for less than $10,000. You're getting a great deal here." Though it might not be obvious at first glance, this is leadership at work. It is prudent leadership on their part, and you have a choice to make in that moment. Will you follow, or will you lead?

Here is another example: Today I took four antique car parts to a shop so that they could be plated with chrome. I know absolutely nothing about the chrome plating industry. And my friendly shop owner studied my parts, frowned, and said, "Oh, this is a tough job. See how detailed these parts are? You can't get these done for less than $250 or $300 each." In fact, I had already tried to get other estimates, and only succeeded in finding one shop which would give me a "ballpark" estimate of $200 each. But I'd need to send the parts to Canada and await a more detailed estimate before they would commit to a price. A good leadership move on their part, I might add! Once they go to the trouble of shipping the parts to Canada, the majority of their customers will simply sign off on the estimate, no matter what the price. Who wants to pay for shipping twice, and still have the problem unsolved? I had a strong suspicion that the real price would go up by 50% if I sent those parts to Canada.

I had a choice to make. I could fold my tent and say something like this to the shop owner: "Ok, so what will you do them for? Is it $250 or $300?" (Want to place your bet on which number he would have given me?) In doing this I would leave him with the upper hand and not challenge his leadership at all. But instead, I decided to take some leadership away from my friendly shop owner. I thought for a minute, smiled and said, "Ok, here's what we can do. I will pay you $850 to do all four of them, and I need two of them in two weeks. The other two you can take as long as you need to. Heck, take six months if you need to. But I need one set right away." It was a gamble, but what did that cost me? Nothing! In asserting my own leadership, I put him back on his heels, but in a friendly way. I took leadership, I was resolute, and I gave him some ground as well. He accepted my proposition almost immediately.

Both of us have had experience in the art of persuasion. Neither of us was or is a hard negotiator, but we do know people and have a natural ability to connect with them relationally. This has saved us many headaches and lots of money, although we still get burned on occasion. This is art, not science.

Some people are natural leaders, and others acquire those skills. But leadership skills are imperative in this business. If you can't lead people, learn to do it or find a partner who can.

A Partner

Do you have a partner? There is great wisdom in sharing the work even if you must share the profit. Real estate is time-sensitive. There are markets to be "hit" at an opportune time, and taxes and interest to pay on a project that you hold for a long time. Those realities demand that you move fairly quickly. And having a good partner can really help speed up the process.

Having a partner also doubles your wisdom. We cannot tell you how many times one or the other of us has caught a detail or provided critical insight that saved us both time and money. We will discuss this later, but having a partner doubles your financing—a critical issue. And not being tradesmen, having a partner has doubled our inventory of tools! It also makes you accountable, which is very good. You don't tend to cut corners when you have another person with a vested interest involved.

Finally, having a partner cuts your risk in half. We haven't experienced a bad outcome on a project yet, but it is always a possibility! And it is nice to know that someone is going to be in this with you if it all turns south.

Of course, having a partner with whom you have fundamental differences would be worse than going into this venture alone. Like a marriage, you need to think this through carefully before you make a commitment because it will either be a great blessing or a real problem! Our partnership is the product of years of friendship. We share common spiritual and ethical values and have an incredibly high trust level with one another. We simply never question who spends money and on what. We do have a notarized working agreement and a joint business account, but our friendship and trust is far more important than those documents and is truly what safeguards our partnership.

In a partnership, as in a marriage, a parting of ways would be difficult and tragic. Do everything in your power before you start to ensure that this will never happen. We certainly do disagree at times, but our mutual respect, shared core values and ability to be both humble and honest with one another has made being in partnership a wonderful experience.

I know that both of us have had at least a couple of fleeting thoughts like, "I could do this by myself and make twice as much!" But the reality is, it would, in most cases, be a nightmare for either of us. The Old Book says, "Two are better than one because they have good return for their labor." Amen.

Strong Common Sense

Would people describe you as a person who has good common sense? Another great asset that we brought to the table at the start was the fact that we are both wise people. We have a track record of good decisions in our personal and business lives, and that translates into great leverage in the home renovation game. There are countless times when you just have to "know" something without being an expert. (The fact that you are reading this book rather than some get-rich-quick scheme speaks well of your ability here!) If something looks too good to be true, it is. Believe that. And be sure to surround yourself with folks who will hold you accountable and tell you the truth.

Winning Track Record

It is said that the best predictor of future performance is past performance. If you handle money well, you will likely handle money well in the future. If you seem to lose at every venture you try, that is not a good sign for future endeavors. Craig has envisioned and built a successful Internet company and has proven himself as a successful business consultant. Jim has a track record of developing people and ministries over 26 years and has a profitable hobby in buying and selling antique cars. Both of us handle money well. We had a track record, and that gave us and our investors confidence that we could at least break even in real estate even if we did not know exactly what we were doing at the start.

Do you have a good track record, even if in a totally unrelated field? Can you balance your check book? Can you deal responsibly with your family's finances? Do you have good credit and a good reputation? Then you are in great shape. But if not, maybe you would be better off building a good track record in a low-risk environment while you learn the ropes.

Here's a quick checklist. This is a very unscientific tool, but if you find yourself on the low end of a number of these indicators, you might want to re-think starting your home renovation career, at least until you can address some of the areas in deficit.

Checklist:

Courage	❏ Low	❏ Average	❏ High
Responsible Risk Taker	❏ Low	❏ Average	❏ High
Good People Skills	❏ Low	❏ Average	❏ High
Leadership	❏ Low	❏ Average	❏ High
Partner (optional, but wise)	❏ Low	❏ Average	❏ High
Common Sense	❏ Low	❏ Average	❏ High
Good Track Record	❏ Low	❏ Average	❏ High

chapter 4

Should You Quit Your Day Job?

If you are wise, you are already asking the question, "How much of my time will this take?" Well, it all depends. If you are reading this book, you are likely not a real estate or building trade professional. That means that you have a lot to learn. For that reason, we would encourage you to think of this as a free-time or part-time endeavor until you gain some experience. In short, don't think about quitting your day job, at least not yet.

The amount of time that a home renovation business will claim depends on a couple of important factors. These include the following:

- **Your level of involvement**—In this venture there is a great deal of difference between being a skilled builder who does most of the work, a handyman who does some work and hires some contractors, a general contractor working close to the project, or an executive who manages from an office.

  We will treat this more fully in another chapter, but in theory, the closer to the builder side of this equation you are, the more time it will demand. And the closer to the executive side of the equation, the more experience it will take.

  Assuming that you are a fairly accomplished handyman (as we were at the start) or even a general contractor, you can plan on spending about 20 hours per week per project in order to complete it in a reasonable amount of time.

Some of those hours absolutely will need to be weekday and daytime hours, since this is when you will meet and monitor your sub-contractors. Other hours may be spent at night or on weekends, as you are able.

- **The scope of the project** — This goes without saying. But ironically, there are similarities in the extreme cases on both ends. The project that requires minimal renovation may not require too much of your own time. But the project that requires a total "gut" may also require less of your time because you will be subcontracting out much of the work.

  We have found that the mid-range projects seem to demand the most of us, because we are reluctant to sub-out those small projects that we can easily do ourselves. We make much more money that way, but we spend much more time.

The bottom line? Figure on working hard, really hard, on your first couple of projects. Unless you have great connections with professional tradesmen or are an incredibly talented at delegation, 20 hours/week is a good projection, to start with. Or maybe 30 hours/week split between you and your partner. You can adjust that time commitment up or down as you figure out your particular gifts, interests and abilities.

chapter **5**

How to Get Financing

It takes money to make money. That's the oldest truism in business. So where do you find the money it takes to buy another house?

It's easier than you might think. Fortunately for you, the Lords of Credit in our culture are all too happy to extend you a hand. But remember, despite what they may tell you, they are not in business to help you or to make you rich. They are in business to take your money and make themselves rich. So engage them and use them, but be as wise as a fox.

The traditional way to purchase a home is by taking out a mortgage. You can certainly do this, but you will run into a couple of problems. First, few lenders want to lend you money on a house that you cannot occupy. And if they do, it will be at a higher rate than a person would pay for a traditional mortgage because for them the loan is a higher risk. Then there will be "points." "Points" are percentage points of the loan you are taking. Two points on a $100,000 loan equals $2,000 in bank fees. Points are a clever way that the mortgage industry characterizes charges which would otherwise be called "exorbitant fees you pay to banks for the privilege of paying high interest on your loan and to compensate a $12/hour secretary for making six copies of the loan documents." But banks call them "points." Genius!

Second, it will take weeks of approvals, inspections, appraisals and more, burning time that you could have spent renovating your home. Third, the person selling you the property must wait until you have all of your approvals before they know that you can and will indeed purchase the property. That puts you at a tremendous disadvantage relative to other buyers who have enough cash to buy the house outright and close the deal quickly. So the trick is, get cash, enough to make a "cash offer" on the home you want to buy. Here are some options.

Home Equity

The banks want you to believe that all of that equity in your home is just sitting there for you to tap to spend on vacations, cars and plasma TV's. Without going into a lesson on economics, using home equity for those things is a bad idea. No, a REALLY bad idea. Do not mortgage a depreciating asset, ever. That is excellent, free advice.

But we discovered that a home equity line of credit, or HELOC, is a wonderful gift to home renovators. It allows you to borrow money instantly, at low rates, and the interest is tax deductible. Both of our homes had significant equity just waiting to be tapped, and we weren't going to use it for a new TV. So we extended our HELOC approvals to the very maximum, with the enthusiastic help of our friendly banker who hoped that we would buy a home entertainment system, or lose our shirts and pay it all back over many years, all the while paying him interest. Silly banker.

We paid a grand total of about $1,200 in interest on our first project. Chump change, in the total scheme of things. And having ready access to $200,000 in cash meant that we could buy the house for cash. What an advantage! We made disbursements from our HELOC's as needed to pay for materials and contractors, and when the project was done, reimbursed our credit lines fully.

Another real advantage of using a HELOC is that if the project turns out to be a total financial disaster, you already have the loss financed. **We would strongly suggest that you keep the scope of your first few projects at level that would not be hard to handle if you lost money.** If we were to lose $50,000 on a project (a total catastrophe), that would mean only the addition of $25,000 to each of our home mortgages. That could be handled by a payment of only $150/month over 30 years at 6%. A problem to be sure, but not a financial catastrophe.

You will find that the banks are glad to extend you as much credit on your HELOC as they are able. Ask them! Just don't go buy that plasma TV when you are approved for your credit line.

Partnership

We mentioned this earlier - having a partner has many advantages. As it relates to financing your project, it doubles the amount of money that you have access to. This is a huge advantage over working alone. To keep it simple we always put in equal amounts of cash every time the business checking account was drawn down. And we found that by paying attention to our personal credit scores (do this at freecreditreport.com or a similar site) we were usually able to fund one large or two moderate projects simultaneously without much trouble by simply borrowing against our HELOC's.

Banks and Business Loans

Banks are delighted to loan you money as long as you don't need money. If you have a long track record of success and tax forms to prove it you will find that getting a loan from a bank a relative breeze.

The problem for most is starting this process. How do we start this business without a loan and how do we develop a track record to prove that we are loan worthy? For us, it started with the use of our home equity lines of credit. We did this for a couple of years until one of our bank officers noticed that we might be a good source of new business. The bank offered us a small business loan. The loan was not very large, but they argued that if we began to develop a solid loan history with the bank the amount we could borrow would increase over time. This small business loan is collateralized on our homes, but rather than us each having access to 90% LTV (loan to value) on our homes we are actually now at 120% LTV. The additional 30% was given to us because of the solid track record we developed while we were using our HELOCs. Without the track record we would have only had access to 90%LTV. This is an incremental method of moving from being a small-time investor to being a big-time investor.

If you are short on home equity and wish to "go big" right off the bat you have your work cut out for you. You will need a business plan written by a professional and a litany of other items.

Here is an excerpt from SBA.gov. (the U.S. Small Business Administration) that describes some of the things you will need to get a small business loan.

Documentation requirements may vary; contact your lender for information you must supply. Common requirements include: purpose of the loan, history of the business, financial statements for three years (existing businesses), schedule of term debts (existing businesses), aging of accounts receivable and payable (existing businesses), projected opening-day balance sheet (new businesses), lease details, amount of investment in the business by the owner(s), projections of income, expenses and cashflow, signed personal financial statements and personal resume(s).

You should take the information, including your loan proposal and submit it to a local lender. If the lender is unable to approve your loan, you may ask if the lender can consider your request under the SBA loan guaranty program. Under this program, the SBA can guaranty up to 85% of a small business loan; however, the lender must agree to loaning the money with the SBA guarantee.

The lender will then forward your loan application and a credit analysis to the nearest SBA District Office. After receiving all documentation, the SBA analyzes the entire application, then makes its decision. The process may take up to 10 days to complete. If the lender needs SBA applications and/or guidance it may contact the nearest SBA District Office by going to http://www.sba.gov/regions/ states.html. Upon SBA approval, the lending institution closes the loan and disburses the funds.

As you can see, simply preparing for an SBA backed loan is a daunting task. We have heard stories of this process taking a very long time—much longer than it takes for us to purchase, renovate and sell a home!

The means that a bank uses to assess your creditworthiness are the money you have in the bank and your credit scores. There are no substitutes for having assets and a good credit history. But those indicators are not the only factors. Your track record as a home renovator may not show up on either your credit score or your bank balance, at least not right away. This is why it is important to communicate with a key person or two at your bank whenever you can. Keep them posted on how your business is going! Underwriters are impersonal and their assessment of your credit is important, but they are not the only determinants of whether or not you will be extended credit. Even as a small customer, you can be seen as a good customer. Banks do like to help local businesses, and you should make sure that you are seen as a contributor to the community good. This can really help your position in terms of available credit and the interest rates you are charged.

Private Investors

We have, on occasion, had the need to borrow beyond what we had available on our HELOCs. In that case we were able to ask a friend for a short-term loan to bridge us until we could close on a property. We weighed the risk and decided that the property we wanted to buy was just too good to pass up. So we went to our friend for help. We offered him a rate that was roughly double the prime rate, feeling that since this was an unsecured loan on his part we should pay him a premium interest rate. Perhaps you have a friend or family member who is willing and able to lend you funds.

Our caution is that such loans are usually unsecured—that is to say that they are not backed up by anything of substance. If catastrophe strikes, you simply won't have the means to pay the loan back. On one hand, it is easier to deal with private investors than it is to deal with banks. But on the other hand, if a bank won't loan you money, you might want to take that as a sign that you are in over your head. Take your time and mitigate your risk. You have plenty of time and opportunities ahead of you. Remember, this is not about getting rich quickly. Slow and steady wins the race.

No matter what source you use for financing your project, be sure that you have access to enough cash for every conceivable expense! You will obviously need access to cash to pay for materials and contractors' services. And do not forget to include your "holding costs" when you calculate the amount of money you need. These costs include monthly interest on any loans you may have taken, property taxes, utilities, insurance, lawn care, snow removal.

In short, any monthly expense that a homeowner might expect to incur, you will incur for a number of months. Do not underestimate the number of months during which you will be paying these costs! Our target is usually to finish a home in three months, maximum, and see it sold in no more than an additional six weeks.But if you should run into unexpected repairs, or if the market flattens out and you end up owning a finished house for six months, could you continue to finance the project? You would do well to overestimate the amount of cash you need access to and then not use it all, rather than having to scramble for capital in the midst of a project!

chapter **6**

How to Study Market Conditions

If you are going to make money in this endeavor, you are going to have to become capable in the field of real estate market analysis. No, you don't have to take a ten week correspondence course, but you will have much to learn. There are lots of factors which will impact which houses you should buy, how much you should pay for them, how much to invest in their renovation, and how much you should sell them for. And you need to become familiar with those factors and the sources of information that help you to understand them.

Read!

You should become familiar with the real estate section of your newspaper. It is often full of great information. For one thing, many local papers list recent real estate transactions weekly. The closing prices of every home in your area may be listed for you to see. Note the prices and the trends!

Another source of information can be the business section of the newspaper and the Wall Street Journal. Real estate is big business, and you will often find great information on interest rate activity and real estate trends. Good information is your best friend. You want as much knowledge as you can accumulate to give yourself every advantage.

Interest Rates

Most of us have at least heard the name "Alan Greenspan"—well get ready to remember another name, Ben Bernanke (the new Fed. chief). He may be your best friend or your mortal enemy depending on what you are trying to accomplish. But one thing is for sure, you need to understand how interest rates affect the real estate market.

Simply stated, when rates are low, people have more buying power. That is part of what has fueled the current real estate boom. A person who could qualify for a loan to finance a $200,000 house at 8% interest rates a few years ago might find that they now qualify for a $300,000 loan at a rate of 6.3%. They have no more income than they did a few years ago, but since rates are lower, they have more buying power.

So what does that do to home prices? It drives them up, of course. And quickly. As more people can afford the seller's home, he will increase the price to gain the most benefit from everyone's increasing buying power. A rising tide lifts all the boats in a harbor. Even distressed properties have seen a tremendous appreciation in price, because when renovated these homes have more value. This is great for sellers, not so great for buyers.

But remember, it's not all bad news for you. You are both a buyer and a seller! So in some respects, interest rates have a minimal impact on your renovation business other than the cost of the money you need to borrow, as long as the rates remain stable.

The real problem comes when rates rise quickly. Let's say the rates spike by a mere 0.5% in the time you are renovating a house. You have paid a premium for a home when the rates were low, and now you have lost thousands of buyers who would have otherwise qualified to buy your home. Let's face it, everyone tends to try to buy as much house as they can qualify for, right? So all those folks on the edge just lost buying power and can no longer buy your house.

What are the implications for you? Well, several. For one, you should try to move in and out of a project as quickly as possible. Buying a low-cost home in a low-tax area with low-interest money may make it tempting to move slowly and take a year to renovate the home. After all, your carrying charges are minimal, right? But it is unlikely that interest rates will ever again hit the historic lows of 2004. Rising rates spell trouble for you if you hold the house for very long. Even if the prices in the neighborhood do not drop, the number of potential buyers likely will.

Rising interest rates may also influence the demographic of the potential buyers. They may make a higher-end project more difficult, but they may make a lower-end project much more desirable and even lucrative for you as buyers ratchet down their expectations. At this writing we are in a climate of rising interest rates. That is one reason why C &W Renovations LLC has continued to target low and middle range houses for renovation. The potential buyer pool is likely to remain larger for longer.

Supply and Demand

Here is another old economic truism: When something is scarce, it is expensive. When it is plentiful, it is cheap. So generally speaking, while buying a house in an area where lots of homes are available may allow you to purchase one cheaply, you will have lots of competition when it comes time to sell it. But the caveat to this law of supply and demand is that when *buyers* are in short supply, home prices stay low even if there are not many on the market.

The trick is to find a house in a scarce market and not pay too much for it. That's your prime target. To find those houses, you will have to do some real research and work closely with a realtor who knows your market well. Your realtor has more experience than you can ever hope to gain. We'll go into more about that shortly, but pay attention to your realtor's expertise!

When You Will Find the Best Prices

Spring and early summer are prime home buying season. Every realtor is busy then and there are lots of homes on the market. Schools are ending, jobs are changing, folks are moving. Even though supply is high, with many potential buyers out there prices are still high and sellers can wait for the maximum price. So remembering the law of supply and demand, when do you want to buy? Not spring and early summer! But when do you want to sell? Spring and early summer, of course!

We have made our best deals when we have bought in the winter and had the renovation ready for sale in the spring. Although houses we want to buy are not plentiful in the winter, they are often for sale at a good price because anyone selling a house at that time is usually motivated to sell and few buyers are looking. Without many buyers and much activity, houses seem to sit on the market for long periods of time and sellers will negotiate. And buying a house in the winter gives you just the right amount of time to complete it and put it on the market in prime time—spring and early summer.

Renovate to Rent

It is not our purpose in this book to give you a complete tutorial on rental properties. We have sold many more properties than we have rented. But we do have some experience in this area that may be useful for you.

There are times when the market conditions warrant renting a home rather than selling it. This is usually when interest rates rise and people's buying power shrinks. In these times it may be an advantage to hold properties for a time and simply rent them. There are both advantages and disadvantages to this approach.

There are significant financial advantages associated with rental properties:

- Keeping a property for over a year allows you to pay the flat capital gains tax, rather than having your profit taxed as income.

- The depreciation allowance and the ability to write off every expense relating to the rental may, in many cases, net you a significant tax loss on your property each year.

- You may gain a regular cash flow from the rental income.

- Appreciation on your property—you can always sell it at another time, presumably for more than you can now.

But there are disadvantages as well.

- Upkeep. Rental properties need regular upkeep, and this can be a major expense if you contract that out. If you attempt to do this yourself, it can be a major headache!

- Damage. You may find yourself needing to re-renovate your home after a few years! Renters are notorious for not taking care of someone else's property. We have bought several properties which have previously been rentals and they were in terrible repair.

- Depreciation in a bad market. It is possible to lose money in real estate! Sometimes a bird in the hand is best. If you can make a profit now, why not sell?

- Keeping it rented. Every month that goes by with the property un-rented is a significant cash drain on you. If you should find yourself "between renters" for a length of time, that could be a real problem.

- Difficulties with tenants. You may have to deal with late or unpaid rent, unreasonable demands, the difficulty of removing bad tenants (a legal nightmare in most states), and a host of other possibilities.

The obvious question when choosing between selling or renting a house is this: will I make enough money to warrant renting the home? But the obvious question does not have a simple answer. There are many factors that determine whether or not this is a good idea, and some of these factors are not financial considerations.

Here are some rules of thumb that you may apply when deciding whether or not holding a home to rent is a good idea.

First, do you live in an area where renting a home is customary? You might not think of this question at first, but in some areas of the country, people tend not to rent single-family homes. Apartments, duplexes, condos and townhouses may be candidates as rental properties, but in some communities you find very few single-family homes being rented. Where we live it is very unusual to find people looking to rent a single-family home unless it is in proximity to a university. So right from the start, our pool of prospective renters is small. However, in some communities it is very common for people to rent homes. Obviously, in that case it might be worth looking into holding a home to rent.

Another rule of thumb is to look at the value-to-rent ratio in your area. For instance, in Richmond, Virginia, a home that sells for $125,000 might bring $1,200/month in rent. That same home in central New Jersey would cost $250,000, but will only bring $1,800/month in rent. Whether you have purchased the property with cash or are holding a mortgage, you have far more money invested in the house in New Jersey, and this differential is not offset by only a 50% increase in rent. As you can see, the rent-to-value ratio is far better in Richmond and by and large, it would be much more profitable to own rental properties in that city.

Property taxes are another factor that influences the profitability of renting a property. To use the same example above, you might expect to pay $6,000/year on the home in central New Jersey, while paying only $2,000 in Richmond. When you add an additional $333/month to your expenses, you have eaten up over half of the difference in rent. So it certainly pays to find rental houses in low-tax areas rather than high-tax areas.

With some exceptions, the people who rent homes long-term are usually blue-collar workers who live more or less paycheck to paycheck. If your home is in a blue-collar area, or an area with factories and production-type industry, you may find more renters looking for an opportunity to rent a home for many years. And long-term renters are generally a better risk for you. They tend to take far better care of the home, and you won't often be looking for new tenants as folks move out.

We would not suggest renting a property if your investment after renovation is more than 80% of the home's value. This is because if you eventually do have to sell it, you are not likely to recoup your investment. You will likely need to spend money on renovating the home again, and you will obviously lose money in realtor's fees and all of the other expenses relating to selling a home.

You should also keep in mind the fact that the best rental properties are in areas which have appreciating real estate values. Your rental home is an asset, and it is not wise to invest in a depreciating asset, even if it is generating an income stream at the present time.

If your home is largely maintenance-free, that would be a helpful factor if you choose to rent it out. Brick homes, homes with vinyl windows and siding, and homes with newer heating systems would all be better candidates for renting than older, maintenance-intensive houses. You will need to either do the maintenance yourself or contract it out, and either way, this is an expensive proposition.

Being a strong negotiator and having a strong personality would be two key character traits you should have if you are considering renting a property. You will need to negotiate a lease, collect late and unpaid rent, confront renters on damage and poor upkeep, and possibly have to evict someone. If you are a "nice guy," you will have difficulty in this arena!

Finally, if you do decide to rent a property, be sure to include every possible regular expense into the lease as the tenant's responsibility. You absolutely do not want to be responsible for paying the heat, gas, water, sewer or electric bills. Being on the hook to pay these bills puts you at the mercy of the tenant in terms of their responsible use of utilities. You also do not want to be responsible for snow removal or lawn care. In short, if you are going to rent a property, you want it to be as simple and painless as possible from the start.

There are software programs available that you can use to ascertain whether or not a particular property is a good candidate for renting. We would suggest that you avail yourself of every resource before you decide to complicate your renovation business with a property rental business. Though there are some similarities, the differences are great enough that we have not felt it wise to venture very far in to this side of the real estate game.

chapter **7**

Know Your Niche

Just what is it that will make your home renovation venture more successful than anyone else's? Well, for starters, you have bought this book. That counts for something. But what else? We believe that you really should try to figure out what your very special angle is.

Great companies find their niche and stay with it. Ford sells cars, and Walmart sells cheap household stuff. What is it that you sell? We at C & W Renovations LLC have pretty much centered on houses in mid-income neighborhoods which need a $30,000 investment. We know where to find them, we know what they look like, and we know how to renovate them and sell them for a good profit. As was discussed in previous chapters, we also have become known as a company that is friendly, works with integrity, and engages the neighborhood. And there are some distinctives of our work: beautiful, well lit kitchens, and nice landscaping. If you saw one of our renovated homes, you would get the picture.

We have been tempted to ramp this up another level and buy some $300,000+ homes, but at least at this point, we want to stick to what we know works. How will you define your work? What kinds of projects will you take on, while leaving others alone? We suggest that you spend some time developing some core values and perspectives that will focus your efforts. You can always change and grow, but it is better to start with an idea and develop it rather than trying to do everything you are able to do.

On the other hand, because we are dealing in the lower range of properties in our area, we have been stung a few times by buyers who have backed out of contracts due to their poor credit and inability to secure financing. That has been one major annoyance of dealing on the lower end of the scale. We would assume that buyers on the mid or upper end of the economic scale probably do not have as many problems of this nature. But then we would likely be dealing with buyers who are much more picky, a larger number of comparable homes, and attorneys who make life miserable. We guess it all balances out in the end!

chapter 8

Who Are My Competitors?

You might be asking, "What does it matter that I know who is out there doing what I am doing?" But it is always helpful to understand who the competition is and how they function. This can give you a leg up on some properties, and it can be a short-cut to help you avoid other homes that would be a waste of your time to bid on.

Teachers

Teachers? Yes, teachers. We are hearing more and more about teachers who are flipping homes to supplement their income. Think about it—many of them are not well paid, they are smart, and most of them have two or three months off in the summer. A great fit for this kind of business! But knowing that they have a particular window of opportunity is helpful. They can only really do this during the summer, which generally means that they will be looking for properties in February through April with hopes of closing in May. You can easily beat that group to the punch if you do hard work looking for properties in the early winter.

Tradesmen

Nearly every time we have looked at a bank-owned home, we have seen a tradesman's truck parked out front or driving away. Really bad homes are great opportunities for plumbers, electricians, masons and carpenters. That is because the labor that you are going to have to pay lots of money for is virtually free for them. They can do their particular trade work themselves or send a crew that would otherwise not be busy and get double value. The good news is that they already have a line of work that will likely keep them busy.

But the bad news is that they can beat the pants off you on a really bad house with their level of expertise and the contacts they may have in other trades. That's another reason why we have avoided foreclosures and bank-owned homes. They are easy for tradesmen to spot and bid on.

Volume Buyers

Trust us, you are not the only one who thinks that renovating homes is a good way to make money. There are lots of folks out there who are incredibly well-financed and who can afford to outbid you. They have paid "bird dogs" to whom they give $1,000 or more per property to identify deals that they eventually close. Even if they make only $5,000 per renovation, they can make it up in volume. That's just what they do. And they're not dirtying their hands like you are.

So how do you beat these guys? You need to outwork them. You need to find the properties that they don't want to spend the time finding! Most of these guys pay a service to compile a list of foreclosures and bank sales. Easy. You will need to work harder than that. Go back and read the previous chapter again. There are deals out there, but you will have to do the leg work that these volume buyers won't do.

Realtors

Realtors are kind of like tradesmen, in that they have an advantage over you in what they know and what they know how to do. They absolutely will have first access to distressed real estate. But most of them can, in this climate, make plenty of money simply selling the homes that others renovate. Real estate laws make it difficult for realtors to function as agents, buyers and sellers all at the same time, so fewer of them are engaged in the renovation business than you might think. Our experience has been that while some realtors buy opportunistically priced homes to rent out, few of them are really interested in substantially renovating them for sale.

This is where your relationship with your friendly realtor offers such a bonus. If you can convince her that you will be more than happy to create a steady stream of listings for her, she may be more than glad to let you do the dirty work of renovating them. That means that she will pass along all of the timely information that she has access to. So keep working on that relationship!

chapter 9

Finding The Right Home
to Renovate

Buying the house to renovate is obviously one of the key moments in the process. Which house should you buy? Generally speaking, if you buy low, control costs and sell high, you will cash out big in the end. We could only wish it was that simple! It's not. There are obviously dozens of questions you need to ask and answer in order to be successful at renovating homes. For starters, how do you know what market will best serve your interests; low, middle or high end? What makes a home a worthy candidate for renovation? How do you find homes to purchase? There are some simple rules to follow and a few tricks to learn that will help you make a smart investment from the start.

Our formula is fairly simple. We look for distressed homes that should sell for the median price in a given demographic area. We buy them for less than the median price, renovate them for a reasonable cost, and sell them for more than the median price. Therein lays our profit margin. The median is where the action is. More homes are for sale and more buyers are looking to buy in the middle of the scale. The trick is buying on the very low end of that median and selling at the very high end of the median.

This formula still leaves an important question unanswered. Which demographic area should you deal with? In every area of the country you will find homes of varying values, usually clustered into small communities with distinct, but often invisible borders. As a resident of a particular area you will know instantly when you have crossed the kind of invisible border that separates one demographic area from another.

It is interesting to note that these areas are not defined by the real dollar values of the homes found within them. Instead, the areas are defined in relative way, more demographically determined than by the real cost of the homes. For instance, a home in a declining neighborhood in New Jersey may have twice the dollar value of a home in an upper middle-class neighborhood in North Carolina, but the New Jersey owner is still thought of as being in a lower demographic.

With this in mind, let's put the real dollar values aside. The decision you must make is this: which kind of demographic area will bring the most opportunity for you? If we were to oversimplify demographic areas into five groups, it would look something like this:

Area 1:
Neighborhoods which are in full decline.

These areas are usually symbolized by vacant row homes, urban decay and crime. In fact, some rural areas also qualify as areas in full decline. But the common factor is this: nobody really wants to buy a home in an area like this unless they are forced by economic circumstances to do so. Few homes are in good shape in this neighborhood.

Area 2:
Neighborhoods which are not in full decline, but could be.

These areas may be declining or may be rebounding. The trick is to figure out which is true. You will need to ascertain whether people are moving in or moving out. An area which is declining is obviously not a place to invest! But an area in distress where the residents are committed to improving the neighborhood may be a great place to buy homes. 50% of the homes in this neighborhood are in good shape.

Area 3:
Neighborhoods in the middle demographic.

As we mentioned previously, income in real dollars is not the issue here. What is at issue is the relative demographic. In these areas, homes are being bought and sold on a regular basis, and residents take pride in their homes. 90% of the homes in this neighborhood are in good shape.

Area 4:
Neighborhoods in the upper-middle demographic.

Homes in areas like this will not remain on the market long. Schools will be very good, if not excellent. Relative incomes will be high, and most residents will be white-collar workers. Anyone who does not carefully maintain the appearance of their home will be ostracized by their neighbors. 98% of the homes in this neighborhood are in good shape.

Area 5:
The upper crust.

This area represents the highest relative demographic in an area. Existing homes may or may not remain on the market long but so few homes are distressed that opportunities are very limited. Nearly 100% of homes in these neighborhoods are in good shape. Even if you are fortunate enough to find a home in need of enough renovation to make it worth considering, the amount of capital you will need to commit will be more than most renovators can handle until they have been in the business for a while. You will need to have nerves of steel to commit $1.2 million to make $100,000.

With this as a background, which area will work best for your renovation business? In our opinion, areas 2 and 3 are the places to invest your efforts. There are many reasons for this.

In many fully declined neighborhoods, "Area 1s," you will be able to purchase houses for next to nothing. Television info-mercials trumpet the fact that you can put ten foreclosed homes on your credit card, and this is absolutely true. But can you sell them when you are finished renovating them? Here is a rule of thumb to remember: if nobody wants to buy these houses wholesale, nobody will want to buy them for retail, either. No matter how much work you put into them, they will still remain in a declined area. And they will not be a good investment unless the entire neighborhood begins to turn around in a significant way. People at any point on the demographic scale simply do not want to purchase properties in areas that they do not consider "safe." They may rent, if necessary. But they will not invest their own money in an area in full decline.

At the other end of the scale, homes in Areas 4 and 5 represent great opportunities, but distressed properties in these areas are extremely scarce. If you are lucky enough to find one you will absolutely stand to make a significant profit. But finding one is nearly impossible. And if you do, you will need to be prepared to invest two, three or even five times as much capital to purchase and renovate the home. Your holding costs will also be far higher in this kind of area. Taxes will be higher, and your monthly interest payment will obviously be higher if you have to invest more money for the purchase. If you are well-financed and patient, go for it! But we prefer to have a steady stream of bronze opportunities rather than wait for one golden opportunity.

Areas 2 and 3 are our bread and butter, and we believe that they will be yours, too. Distressed homes are plentiful, your initial investment will be modest, and many potential buyers will be at the ready when you are finished with the renovation. Areas 2 and 3 also have well established property values. There will be trends that you can track and "comps" that you can evaluate. These are things that help you to determine what you should pay for a house and what you might reasonably expect to sell it for when you are finished renovating it. You will not have quite the volume that is possible in Area 1, nor the net profit you might have in Areas 4 and 5. But you will have many opportunities to successfully renovate homes for a decent profit.

There is a basic profile of the home you should be looking for in Areas 2 and 3. First, it should have a minimum of three bedrooms. Few buyers will consider purchasing a home which does not have at least three bedrooms because most buyers in these areas have, or plan to have, more than one child. You should also look for homes that have more than one full bathroom. In most demographics, bathrooms are very important as "personal space." Parents don't like to share bathrooms with kids if they can avoid it. And if there are more than two children in a home, a home with a single bathroom may be totally impractical.

You should also look for homes that have a good floor plan. We almost always disqualify homes with strange or impractical outside access, isolated bedrooms, or unworkable kitchen layouts unless we can easily remedy these issues. If there is an inexpensive and practical way to improve the home's floor plan, we may be looking at a great opportunity rather than a losing proposition. But make sure you know the difference!

We also tend to avoid buying homes that have poorly conceived or badly constructed additions. We recently passed on one home because we were unsure of the integrity of the construction of a porch that had been turned into a family room. Although it looked like a bonus at first glance, we suspected that it had been roughed together by an amateur over a long weekend. We may very well have had to remove the entire structure if we had found that it was unstable, unsafe, or far below mechanical standards.

Badly finished basements are another yellow flag for us. That "reclaimed space" may be hiding a moist or leaking foundation wall, improper wiring, or other significant issues. If we are comfortable with the possibility that we might have to turn the space back into a work area rather than a living space, we might still consider the purchase. But anything that looks like the homeowner may have done a sub-standard job give us serious pause as we evaluate a property to purchase.

Another thing we consider when evaluating a home is its age. A home that is older than 50 years is apt to have bad or inadequate wiring, galvanized plumbing, and possibly a suspect foundation. This is not to say that old homes do not represent a good opportunity at times. There are many old homes that are absolutely charming. The architecture is incomparable, the attention to detail is often stunning, and the floor plans may be spacious.

But the heart of a home is its mechanical systems — plumbing, electrical and heating. And in very old homes, unless there have been upgrades over the years, you may be looking at a huge amount of work to renovate the home to a level where you can sell it. This will mean time and money, two commodities that you necessarily need to keep to a minimum if your project is to be profitable.

Find the Ugly Duckling

When we start talking about selling your house after renovation, we will talk about the "Wow Factor." But right now, let's talk about the "Ugh Factor." It just might be the key to your success.

Picture 1
Holly—before

One of the best deals we ever made began when Craig drove down a street in a nice lower-middle income neighborhood. He saw a house with a For Sale sign in the front yard. Oh, he'd seen maybe 200 For Sale signs in front of houses that month. But this one was different and this time he stopped to look. The house on Holly was painted a hideous mint green, the crumbling concrete front walk extended only half-way down to the street, most of the front yard had been overtaken by vines resembling an Amazon rainforest, and the picture window had cracked panes and rotted wood clearly visible from the street.

Ugh. No, double-ugh. Absolutely hideous. And Craig instantly knew that this was a property we just had to buy.

Picture 2
Holly—after

The exterior was only a tip-off. The real nightmare lay inside the front door. This house was worse inside than it was outside, but even so, most of the trouble was cosmetic.

We purchased that property for $165,000, invested less than $20,000 in repairs and upgrades, another $9,000 in a brand new heating and central air conditioning system and sold it for $245,000 in three months. And frankly, the buyer got a steal. That was one NICE house!

We were proud as could be, and the neighbors nominated us for Mayor. But it was the ugly duckling in the neighborhood. That's what we look for - ugly houses. The uglier the better. Ugly is only skin deep and usually pretty cheap to remedy. But ugly stops most

Picture 3
*Diamond in
the rough on
Osgood Lane?*

folks, who do not have courage or vision, from ever entertaining
the idea of buying a house that looks that bad.

The converse of Holly was Osgood Lane. Osgood Lane was
beautiful. It was a "For Sale By Owner" that I knew we just HAD

Picture 4
Beautiful
woodwork at
Osgood

to buy because it had such wonderful curb appeal, expansive rooms, and marvelous oak trim throughout. And it was cheap, too!

But upon closer scrutiny we found it also had mechanical and structural problems that would have cost us well over $50,000 to remedy before we could even begin a cosmetic renovation. What seemed by all outward appearances to be a beautiful house would have been a nightmare to renovate because it had such significant internal problems.

We passed on that one and looked for an ugly house to renovate!

So repeat after me: Ugly is good. Ugly is good. Ugly is good. And if your spouse has a weak stomach, be sure not to let him or her look at those houses before you purchase them. Jim made that mistake a couple of times and had to do some fast talking to get his wife's endorsement to risk their family's financial security on something that looked like an absolute disaster at the start.

Learn to Study Comparable Properties

You should absolutely know what the value of a particular kind of house in a particular kind of neighborhood is, almost without looking at comps. You will know this information because you have already studied the comps diligently. You know that a 3/1 (3 bedroom, 1 bath) in neighborhood "X" is worth $210,000 - $220,000. And when you see one being listed for $175,000, you know you have a potential buy. You can leave that science up to your real estate agent, but practically speaking, you have to be able to make that assessment more quickly than that.

Study the real estate page in your newspaper. Since you probably will not have access to MLS, the multi-listing service that realtors use, Realtor.Com can be a helpful tool, too. Develop a "feel" for neighborhoods relative to home sizes. When your realtor runs comps, print them out and keep them for later reference. You will be glad you did.

Your Realtor Should Be Busy Running Comps!

A "comp" is a "comparable property." The key here is that the house you are using for comparison needs to really be comparable. Not two miles away, not having one more or one less bathroom or bedroom, not having a pool or a 20' white swan statue in the front yard. Insist that your realtor find you REAL comps. They are out there. It is great if you can find recent comps that will pinpoint your eventual selling price. And it is helpful to find comps on bad, dated and distressed properties as well.

As your realtor finds and considers comps, be sure that she generates some comps from two, three or even four years ago. These prices may not be of much value to you in terms of pricing the house today, but they will show you definite trends; whether or not the homes in that particular neighborhood have been increasing in value as quickly as those in other neighborhoods in your area. You obviously want to try to buy homes in areas that have shown a strong historical price increase.

Those comps will inform you on both your purchase price and your eventual selling price, thus giving you a great sense of the "spread" that you are working with. If we don't see a $50,000 spread, we are usually not interested. That is because we have never invested less than $25,000 in renovation on a property, and when we add commissions, carrying charges and a healthy over-run factor, we're going to find that we have invested as much as $40,000 invested really quickly.

DOM—A Wonderful Number

DOM is "Days On Market." And that wonderful number can create a ton of leverage for you when you buy a property. Your realtor can easily check how many days a property has been on the market. That number is listed in MLS in a little section at the bottom of the listing that says, "DOM: xx"

Ask your realtor what the average DOM is in your area. As of this writing, we are told that the average DOM in our area is about thirty days. But when you get down to specifics, the nice houses tend to last only about ten days on the market. So what does that tell you?

Well, a house that has been on the market for over 30 days is usually either overpriced or in need of repairs that the average buyer cannot or does not wish to make. In either case, unless the seller is just "trying out the market," he is rapidly becoming desperate because he knows that his house should have sold by now. That is what we call a "motivated seller." And that is the kind of seller you want to find. When dealing with a motivated seller, you instantly have the upper hand in negotiations.

"TLC"

We love to search by "TLC." It means, "tender loving care" needed. Sometimes that means only that the kitchen is dated and there is a hole in a wall that the buyer does not have time to fix. Other times it means that the whole house needs to be gutted. Either way, it is a signal that the seller is not willing to do what it takes to get maximum value out of the house. And you are! What a happy coincidence!

Ask your realtor to do an "advanced search" using "TLC" as a search criterion. Or scan the newspapers for FSBOs with that term, or perhaps the moniker, "handyman special." Those are prime targets for you to purchase.

Corporate Sales and Foreclosures

We must be honest, other than one stellar success story, we have not had much luck in this area. We have bid on and lost a bunch of these. If you check the infomercials and Internet real estate gurus, you will find them all chanting a mantra about government sales, tax sales and foreclosures. And we're sure that there is money to be made there. The trouble is, that seems to be where everyone, especially the renovating pros, look for deals.

Another problem is that dealing with a bank is not like dealing with "real people." It can be mind-numbing to try to figure out what the protocol is, when bids are acted on and what kind of numbers they expect.

In our experience it has been difficult to actually talk to a human being once we submit a bid. And we major in talking to humans. That's where we do our best work. What seems to happen is that some bank board (or maybe it's all done by computers... who knows?) looks over all of the offers and chooses one. They do not have the time or interest in talking with you or negotiating with you.

If you have great success in this area as a source of homes to renovate, let us know. Maybe we will include your chapter in our next revision of this book. But we believe that you can have just as much success and more fun dealing with humans.

Your Friendly Mail Carrier

How can your friendly mail carrier help you? Well, who else knows which homes are vacant? We know of three mail carriers in one town alone who are in the home renovation business because they have an inside track on good homes to purchase. So the next time your wife tells you that you should give your mail carrier a tin of cookies at Christmas, listen to her. She just might make you some money as you develop a friendship with a person who is a great source of inside information!

Cold Calling

I'm sure that you have received a million cards from your friendly neighborhood realtor asking you if you'd like to sell your home. Well, there is a reason why those cards are mailed. There is some, however small, return rate on that kind of investment. And there is nothing stopping you from contacting the owner of an abandoned or run down house and asking, in a friendly and engaging way, if they would like to sell you their home.

And did you know that you can check tax records to uncover the owners of vacant properties? You just might be doing someone a favor if you make an offer. And you can always knock on a door or leave a note. Very little invested on your part, but it could pay off big!

Newspapers

Once in a while you will see a handyman special listed in the paper, and if someone is dredging for business in the classified section, chances are that they are trying to save a buck. That could work for you or against you. On one hand, that person is not likely to be paying a realtor a commission, and perhaps you may find yourselves splitting the difference in the savings.

On the other hand, this person may be trying to squeeze every dollar out of a property and is not a good prospect to negotiate with. They also may have an inflated idea of the value of their home since they are not working with a realtor. But it never hurts to check! We have found a couple prospects that way.

chapter **10**

Should I Use a Realtor
or Not?

To be successful in this endeavor, you are going to have to spend some money. And one place that your money will be well spent is on a realtor. Sure, there is a movement afoot to drive the "greedy realtors" out of business. FSBO (for sale by owner), Foxtons (2% sales commissions!) and discount realtors are all the rage. As real estate prices have soared and the increase has outpaced inflation by a factor of hundreds and thousands, many people today are wondering if perhaps they are grossly overpaying a realtor who charges a 6% commission to sell a $500,000 house.

After all, many houses in today's market sell in days or weeks and the transactions may be relatively simple. We will not defend realtors and their 6% commissions. In some cases, the seller is not getting his money's worth. But you are not a resident seller. You are in a different ballgame altogether. And you want and need a realtor's help. You need to find a good realtor - one who will work hard for you and be honest with you.

As we mentioned earlier, a reputable realtor who has been in business for a while has more knowledge than you can ever hope to gain. Your realtor knows the neighborhoods. She knows the historic prices, the ebbs and flows. She knows a good street from a bad street on a questionable block. You do not. And your realtor has one other advantage. The Mighty MLS.

MLS? Yes, the secret society of the Multiple Listing Service. Your realtor is certified and has paid a fee to use this service. And she can check historic prices on any house that has sold in any neighborhood for the last five years. What a great tool to have! Before you buy your property, your realtor can tell you with reasonable certainty just what you can expect to sell it for when you are done.

We were very fortunate that in the beginning we connected with a realtor who knows the lower and middle tier housing in our area better than just about anyone. And we quickly established a win-win relationship with her. She would find us good prospects for renovation and we would use her as a buyer's agent, thus netting her a 1.5% to 3% commission out of the seller's pocket, not ours.

Then we would agree to list the property with her after renovation, netting her another commission on the other end. But we do not pay her 6%. We usually pay only 3% if she finds the buyer within her network, and 4.5% if she has to give a point or two to the buyer's agent. This is a real win-win. She makes a total of 4.5% to 6% on the property in the end, receives consistent listings from us, and we benefit from all of her hard work, marketing and experience. It's a beautiful thing.

We have been fortunate to be able to negotiate reduced commissions with our realtor, and you may not be so fortunate. But even if you have to pay a full 6% commission on the homes you sell, you need a realtor who is truly working with you and who wants to continue a productive relationship with you. Consider that money that the realtor makes as money well spent.

Once we were tempted to buy a FSBO property and went so far as to make an offer and have an engineering inspection done. In the end we did not purchase the house because of issues uncovered in the inspection, but our realtor was beside herself when she found out that we were considering the purchase. Not because a FSBO cut her out of half of the deal, but because she knew that this was a bad neighborhood for us to buy in.

She told us she was up all night worrying that we would make a mistake and buy the house and was relieved when she found out that we did not. She made us promise never do to that again, but to ask her advice even if she was not going to earn a commission on a FSBO. That's the kind of realtor you want. Joan has counseled us to pass on several houses that we would have otherwise purchased. We are still a bit mystified as to why she wanted us to pass on a couple of them, but we trust her judgment because she's the pro.

We have now developed such a great relationship with our realtor and her staff that they call us whenever they have a good prospect, even when we are not looking for properties. The better your relationship, the more likely they are to go the extra mile for you.

The real estate industry has come up with an ingenious idea called a "buyer's agent." If you sign an agreement to engage a realtor as your buyer's agent, you will be obligated to make your purchase through him alone. You will not be free to pursue properties that may appear on your radar unless you work through your agent. We find this practice to be wonderful for realtors, but a disadvantage for both buyers and sellers. Why should you forfeit your ability to buy a property that is being listed by another agent? And why should your agent get a percentage of the commission on a property that he had nothing to do with finding for you?

When we have been selling a home, we have also encountered buyers' agents. And our results have not been good. The buyer's agent is apt to lead the buyer to properties that will net them the highest commission, right? And if your selling agent is discounting your commission, as ours sometimes does, she will not have as much money to give back to the buyer's agent. If the buyer does not have an exclusive contract with that agent, this is not a problem.

The agent will take what he can get because the buyer is free to do whatever he wants and may even find another agent. But if the contract is exclusive, the agent may very well dissuade the buyer from bidding on your property, hoping to find one on which he will net a greater commission. This has happened to us, and we were not pleased. For the reasons we have just enumerated, we make it our standard practice to never sign an exclusive buyer's agreement with a realtor.

Remember as you make offers on homes that you intend to purchase that although your realtor is working for you, she actually stands to make more money if you offer more money for a home. This is because she will get a commission off of a higher sale price, and more importantly, if you offer more money there is a higher likelihood that the seller will accept your offer, thereby guaranteeing her a commission. So as you can see, you will need to develop a trusting relationship with your realtor so that you can be confident that if she is counseling you to increase your offer, it is for the right reasons.

Find a good realtor. Find someone who knows your area well, has a lot of experience and a good network, and who has the time and personality to work with you. You might have to try to work with a few different realtors until you find the right one for you, but in the end you will be glad you did!

How to Estimate the Cost of Renovating a Home

Next to the purchase price, estimating the cost of renovation is the most important factor for you to consider. There are actually two issues in play here: 1) what exactly will you change, repair or upgrade, and 2) what will this cost. We'll tackle each of these separately.

What to change?

There will certainly be homes that you could buy that will lend themselves to major renovation. Things like an addition, a second floor, a porch or patio, an additional bathroom, etc. We have seen homes that, with a major addition, could possibly net $100,000 more than they would without it. But when considering major additions, you really need to take several factors into consideration.

What is the cost? Unless you have considerable trade skills, major additions cost much more than you might think. You will save some money over the typical homeowner doing the same thing because you will be acting as your own General Contractor. But a major addition will add much in terms of time, red tape, expense and general headaches. In most cases we have decided to do an excellent job on the renovation and leave major changes for the new homeowner. The new owner can see and appreciate the home's potential. Remember, your task is to make a fair profit in a relatively short period of time, not squeeze every possible dollar out of the project. By doing a major addition you might not be wasting money, but you will likely be wasting time.

It is also possible to over-improve a house based on the neighborhood. Your goal should be to make the house one of the nicest in the neighborhood, but not necessarily the best or biggest house in the neighborhood. That's because of the first axiom in real estate—"it's all about location." Investing a ton of money in major improvements to a house in a certain neighborhood does not change the kind of buyer who is looking in that neighborhood. You may very well price the house right out of the neighborhood and have a terrible time selling it. In an area that is full of 3 bedroom / 1 ½ bathroom houses (3/1.5 in real estate terminology), adding on and creating a 5/3 might be a waste of time and money.

However, if a 2/1 house in that same neighborhood has a nice piece of property and can easily be made into a 3/2, that might be a good improvement to make. There certainly are improvements that will be worth both your time and your money. The question you must ask is, "What is the impact?" New space counts, but so does an excellent renovation of the existing space. If you are going to add high-dollar items, be sure that they count. The rule of thumb in real estate is that kitchens and bathrooms sell houses.

Unlike the unethical flippers who simply put on a coat of paint, we believe that in the long run, under-improving a house is a waste of your time. You want to build a reputation, and you want to market a house that you can be proud of. We do not put $12,000 cabinets in a $180,000 house in a blue collar neighborhood, but neither do we install the cheapest we can find. Quality matters to everyone. In a higher end neighborhood, you will need to use materials that are commensurate with what people are using in their homes there. Perhaps high grade counter tops rather than Formica, tile floors rather than vinyl, etc.

So here's a quick list of the things that we believe are high-impact improvements. These are roughly in descending order of importance but are all critical. They are the things that you should really plan on improving in order to have the kind of traffic and buyers you will want in the end. Don't cut corners on these, and remember to keep the materials used consistent with most homes in the area:

- Kitchens

- Bathrooms (consider adding or modifying one if there are not 2 full baths per 3-4 bedrooms)

- Paint, both interior and exterior

- Floors (new carpet or finished hardwood in living areas, tile or vinyl in kitchen and bath)

- Landscaping

- Windows (people are looking for energy efficiency in most areas today)

- New heating system

- Central air conditioning

Absent from the list above are such things as new second stories, garage conversions, porches, etc. We feel that adding quality tends to win out over adding space most of the time.

Estimating Costs

This is a tricky subject. It is very hard for us to project your costs because there are so many variables. Gutting and rebuilding a bathroom in a $220,000 house might cost half of what it would cost to do a bathroom in a $400,000 house just five miles away in a different neighborhood because the materials and the layout might vary significantly. And renovating identical bathrooms in Little Rock, Arkansas and Greenwich, Connecticut would be worlds apart too, especially if are employing a contractor!

You might start by going to your local home improvement store and buying the latest contractor's guide to pricing home improvement jobs. These are weighted geographically, and should be of some help to you. As you gain experience in your particular niche, you will be able to do this "on the fly." But remember to estimate high! It is always a nice surprise to save money. Underestimating a project is never a nice surprise.

This probably goes without saying, but if you are doing the work yourself, you need only estimate the cost of materials. Otherwise, the more experience you have with contractors, the more easily you will be able to assign a cost for renovating the home before you purchase it. It is possible, as long as you have time to haggle with your seller, to get contractors to give you general estimates or perhaps even firm bids for some of the component parts of the renovation before you make your offer on the house. Either way, it is really imperative that you have a firm grasp on your total renovation cost before you buy!

CHAPTER 11   **HOW TO ESTIMATE THE COST OF
RENOVATING A HOME**

Remember, too, that not every estimate is the same. You would
not be well advised to believe the low bidder on a job every time.
Sometimes contractors can begin a project knowing full well that
they have given you an unrealistically low number and figuring
that they will simply "find an undiscovered problem" and charge
you more in the end. We have had contractors present us with
itemized charges for making trips to Home Depot, as well as
charges for things that any reasonable person would think were
part of the job from the start. This is where developing a cadre of
trusted contractors is invaluable.

And unless you know someone beforehand, it can be a slow and
expensive learning process. Until you gain some experience, be
sure to add 10% to your budget for every contractor's estimate.
That will protect you from some of the inevitable cost over-runs
that they will pass on to you.

We also use a little device called the "Cunningham Factor." This
is named after Jim Cunningham, who always seems to spend at
least 20% more money and 80% more time than he had planned
on the projects he undertakes, be that changing the oil in his
car or digging a post hole. After we total up every conceivable
expense, we add *an additional 30% of the total renovation cost* as
a "Cunningham Factor."

This covers all of the little things that are nearly impossible to
account for at the start—the dozens of $36.04 trips to Home Depot
to buy small items, a few little things we have inevitably forgotten,
and the potential cost over-runs on larger renovation expenses. The
Cunningham Factor also ensures that if we have a nasty surprise

when we open a wall (hidden rot, bad plumbing, faulty wiring and the like) we have a cushion to fall back on. The last thing that the Cunningham factor covers is the cost of opportunities we might have not considered at the start—space we had not noticed where a cool kitchen pantry could fit, an opportunity to add another cabinet here or there, or perhaps a semi-finished basement room that we had not thought of when we bought the house. We have never failed to spend 100% of the Cunningham Factor on a job!

Although you will be tempted to reduce it, The Cunningham Factor is not something to skimp on in your original estimate. It may be a lifesaver for you. And if your skills in estimating the work to be done are exemplary, the Cunningham Factor may either represent "free money" you can spend on an extra touch to make your renovation even more spectacular, or else a nice bonus in your eventual profit.

We have developed a spread sheet that helps us to put all of our costs, both best and worst case scenarios, in one place. This sheet is available in the private side of our website to folks who have purchased this book. We simply plug in our target purchase price, our estimated "holding charges" (interest, taxes, insurance, utilities), real estate commission charges, and the cost of every renovation expense. The Cunningham Factor is automatically calculated as 30% of the total renovation cost. The bottom line shows up as our estimated profit. Without putting it on a spreadsheet, below is an example of how we figured one modest project:

Purchase + Repairs

Purchase	165,000
Closing	1,000
Inspection	200
Interest/taxes/ins (Holding)	6,964
Sub Total	173,164

Repairs

Electric upgrade	480
Exterior(not roof)	
Sidewalks	667
Roof	
Landscape	848
Windows	2,811
Kitchen, including appliances	2,920
Hauling	958
Heater	8,436
Floors	0
Walls	0
Bathroom	3,136
Painter	3,550
Cunningham factor (30%)	7,142
Sub Total	30,947

Total Purchase + Repairs	204,112

Sale - Costs

Sale price	240,000
Closing costs	0
4.5% Commission	-10,800
Home warranty	0
	229,200

	Profit	**25,088**

Notice that we added in our "holding costs" which include interest, taxes and utilities for four months, at least. Those costs can be easily overlooked. In our case we have a relationship with a realtor which allows us to pay a reduced commission. So for the realtor's commission we use a figure of 4.5% which is the most we will be charged, knowing that we might only be charged 3% if our realtor finds the buyer herself. We also add in closing costs (mostly on the front end) which include title insurance and other fees, the cost of our home inspection, insurance, and a home warranty (which we do not always offer). On the revenue side, we use a conservative estimate of the sale price which is always backed up by a competitive market analysis done by our realtor. This generates our estimated profit.

In the early days, we thought a potential profit of $15,000 divided by two was pretty impressive. We were prepared to bid on homes that showed only a $15,000 potential return on our spreadsheet. Then we learned how easy it would be to under-estimate the cost of a project by as much as $20,000. Now we usually do not become involved in a renovation unless our worst case scenario shows at least a $30,000 profit. By being conservative, we have almost always come out ahead of this projection. But we always keep in mind how easy it would be to have our winning streak come to an end!

How Much Should I Offer to Pay for the House?

CHAPTER 12 **HOW MUCH SHOULD I OFFER TO PAY FOR THE HOUSE?**

You should be prepared to make a bit of a paradigm shift from how you may have thought about homes before you went into the real estate business. In our culture, homes are a personal statement. If you insult someone's home, you have insulted them. You might not think about it, but you have been indoctrinated to indulge and approve of people's homes and not criticize their condition or décor. And in all probability you have also been conditioned to care deeply about the home you own.

Our advice to you is, *get over it*! This is business! You will need to prepare yourself to be cold and critical as you assess a home to purchase. To make a good deal you will need to enumerate every flaw and deficiency to the seller. When you make an offer it is a business proposition with someone you do not know. If you "insult" him with a low offer—good. His realtor will advise him that this is business and he needs to counter-offer at $xxx to make the sale. Also remember that you are not buying the home in "move in condition." The seller should assume that he will be somewhat "insulted" by prospective buyers if he is listing a home that is in need of significant renovation.

You will also need to treat the homes you will sell as objects, not as treasured possessions. Once you have invested three months' worth of sweat and blood in a home's renovation, it will feel like your own home. But remember, it isn't! It is an object that is earning you money. Making this paradigm shift is one of the best ways for you to function effectively in the world of buying and selling real estate.

In this business you initially act as a buyer, then eventually as a seller. You are going to have to get used to working both sides of the street in this regard. That is good news for you—you will gain experience as a buyer that will help you as a seller, and vice versa.

You have identified a house for sale that seems to be in a condition that suggests that it would be worth renovating for profit. You have taken a walk through, taken copious notes and arrived at a ball-park figure of what it will cost you to bring it up to the point where it will be attractive to buyers. You have received comparable listings from your realtor and now have a good idea of the potential sale price once the house is renovated. The last piece of data that you need to fit into your calculations is the purchase price. And all that is left is for you to convince the seller that he needs to sell you the house for as little as possible.

In most cases, the ability to purchase the house for a figure that is significantly below the asking price is the most important factor in determining your net profit. Think of difference between the asking price and your eventual purchase price as the easiest money you can make on the property. You may need to negotiate a bit, but you won't have to deal with a contractor or even break a sweat to make $5,000, $10,000 or even $30,000, instantly!

Until you have sold a house or two, it may be difficult for you to enter into the mind of the seller. But this is the frame of reference you must have in order to successfully negotiate a great deal. What are the seller's priorities? Price is a priority, obviously. Nobody wants to sell a house for less than it is really worth. And your seller wants to make every dollar he can. You have no advantage in this department… the seller wants your money and the only way you can help him is to give it to him. That's an obvious disadvantage for you. But the seller has other priorities that you may not be thinking of and this is where you may be able to gain an advantage. Let's take a look at those other priorities.

Speed is a priority. In the majority of cases, once someone puts their house up for sale for any reason, he wants it to be sold as soon as possible. Your seller may be relocating and may already have another house under contract with the sale of his house as a contingency. That puts him in a terrible position, since his contract to purchase could vaporize if he does not sell his present house quickly. The seller's need for speed is your ally. If you are in a position to offer a cash purchase then you may be able to promise the seller that he will have cash in hand within two to three weeks. Be sure that your realtor trumpets this fact to your seller. Even if the seller receives a legitimate offer and accepts it, every month that goes by between the day the house is put under contract and the day the transaction is finalized is costing him a month's mortgage, 1/12 of his tax bill, utilities and insurance.

Plus, the seller must deal with the anxiety caused by the knowledge that the contract may be voided for any number of reasons, leaving him to start the selling process all over again. The prospect of a quick sale may be attractive enough to save you tens of thousands of dollars. As sellers, we give consideration to lower offers if the buyer can close the deal quickly. We know how it feels when a house is under contract but the closing date is months away. Those are anxious months. We know that many things can, and often do, go wrong. So when a buyer promises a quick transaction, we listen!

Buyers who have in their hands a letter which pre-qualifies them for a mortgage are great folks to deal with. We do not have to wonder whether or not we will have to tie up our property under contract while the buyer's credit is assessed. This principle works in reverse as well. As a buyer you should have some certification ready that proves that you are able to make a purchase. This will often motivate a seller to deal with you rather than someone who has made a higher offer but whose proof of funds is lacking. We have won a number of offers because we offer cash and a two-week closing.

Another priority for the seller is the ease of the transaction. When a house is sold it must usually be inspected by the municipality in order to secure a certificate of transfer or occupancy. As a renovator, you have the luxury of offering to buy the home "as is." This can save the seller both time and money. The seller knows with an "as is" sale there will be no further negotiating of the price due to failed inspection issues.

When you sell your first house you will learn what an important motivation this is for the seller. The municipality may present the seller with a list of things that need to be fixed before the transaction can be completed. Some of these repairs may take more time than the seller has to spend. And buyers often produce a list of dozens of small, medium and large demands right at the last minute because they know that by the time the house gets close to the final closing date the seller is at a significant disadvantage.

CHAPTER 12   **HOW MUCH SHOULD I OFFER
TO PAY FOR THE HOUSE?**

When you have sold a few houses, you will be familiar with this
reprehensible tactic used by buyers!

By communicating to your seller that you intend to buy the house
with no further questions asked and no certificate of occupancy
needed, you save him a tremendous amount of trouble and worry.
This is another advantage to the seller that you should be careful to
communicate as you make an offer to purchase.

We should insert a quick caveat here; we never agree to purchase
a house *totally* "as is." We do include *one* contingency in the offer
to purchase. This contingency is that we must have an engineering
report done, at our expense, before we sign the contract. This
protects us from an unnoticed but potentially catastrophic
structural or mechanical issue. When making the offer we are
careful to communicate that we do not anticipate withdrawing our
offer for any of the obvious flaws the house has, no matter how
hideous they may appear. But we do reserve the right to withdraw
the offer if we have missed something truly significant.

It may be naïve on our part, but we try to avoid using attorneys
whenever possible. Although in some parts of the country it would
be almost unthinkable to go to a closing table without an attorney,
we fail to see the necessity in most cases. In most instances, your
realtor and title company are perfectly capable of handing a real
estate closing. Call us crazy for believing this, but isn't that what
they do every day of the week? You will sign dozens of forms
at the closing table, and each and every form is a memorial to a
lawsuit over some particular disagreement that was settled many
years ago.

You now have forms to sign so that lawsuits do not reoccur over those same disagreements. These forms provide plenty of protection for both the buyer and the seller. People buy and sell houses every day and the industry has a pretty good handle on how to do it without exposing the buyer or the seller to legal action. How many more issues could possibly be left that a $500/hour attorney can protect you from?

The point here is that by avoiding attorneys you can un-complicate the transaction for your seller, which is a bonus for him. Put yourself back into his shoes for a minute. Would you rather sell your house to someone who is working through an attorney, or to someone who will deal with you personally?

We once sold a two bedroom, one bath home in a lower-end neighborhood for $185,000. Although that might be a tidy sum in some places, in this town it was the cheapest single family home sold that year, by tens of thousands of dollars. Yet the buyer employed an attorney who treated this transaction as if the buyer was purchasing Trump Plaza. We signed a dozen addendums to the contract, negotiated a long list of demands pertaining to the condition of the house, and after three months of this nonsense the contract was voided by the buyer. It seems that the attorney dragged the process out for so long that the buyer ended up getting cold feet. We lost three months of prime-time marketing and continued to accrue interest and taxes mostly because the buyer's attorney wanted to act like F. Lee Bailey.

And frankly, the buyer lost out, too. His attorney made the transaction so complicated that he was terrified to buy the home.

CHAPTER 12   **HOW MUCH SHOULD I OFFER
TO PAY FOR THE HOUSE?**

We re-listed the property and sold it for the same price to a nice
young couple who did not employ an attorney, and we closed the
deal in a month. Our realtor ran into them two months later and
they were beaming. They absolutely love their house.

This experience has given us great appreciation for the seller who
wants to make a quick, simple sale! Communicate to the seller
that you anticipate making a "title company closing" and assume
that by giving the seller an advantage in speed and ease, you have
created a financial advantage for yourself.

Most sellers have some significant degree of attachment to their
home. They usually would prefer that their home be purchased by
someone who will respect both the property and the neighborhood.
Although you might not think of this as a priority for the seller,
it is, and it can work to your advantage. We go out of our way to
communicate in a friendly, engaging way with the seller, or, if we
are not able to meet him, with his realtor. We make an effort to get
the message back to the seller that we are reputable and honest,
and that our intention is to restore the property to its potential
and create a benefit for the whole neighborhood. This is not a
game for us. We truly do care about the seller, his house and the
neighborhood. But we want to be sure that he knows this. You
might be surprised how important this can be to a seller and how
much this can work in your favor when it comes to dollars and
cents.

Now that you have a good understanding of the seller's priorities
and how you can accommodate them, you are ready to make an
offer. We have heard realtors say things like, "Assume that the

house is priced to sell," and, "Don't insult the seller with a low offer." Hogwash. As sellers ourselves, we price our homes to sell and we don't like to be insulted. Even so, we have other priorities besides price alone, and, we understand that in the end, the market sets the price.

We have never felt insulted by a low offer. Amused, perhaps. But not insulted. We do not become angry, cry, or refuse to deal any further with a potential buyer who makes a low offer. We are quite comfortable simply making a counter offer. Or, if the initial offer is absolutely laughable, we do not respond at all and we wait for a more reasonable offer. But we do not fault buyers for trying!

The lesson here is this: do not be afraid to make a low offer, even an offer that might appear to be ridiculous. You do not know the seller's position or his motivation. He may very well be grateful to receive your low offer. You are not "stealing money" from him by making a low offer. The seller has every right to reject your bid, and he will certainly do so if he believes that he could or should receive more money for the property.

A practical rule of thumb is that if you find that your initial offer is accepted, you may have offered too much! We would advise that you prepare yourself for rejection. If you are not receiving rejections on a regular basis, you may be overestimating the value of the houses you are bidding on.

The realtors on both ends of the transaction will benefit if you make a high offer. Your realtor knows that it is more likely that the seller will accept the offer, thus netting her a sale and a

commission. And, of course, the seller's realtor wouldn't mind
fielding an offer that motivates the seller to make the deal! But you
are not in this business to make money for realtors. Your initial
offer should be bona fide, but low.

How low? It is hard to say. But unless we know that the house
is tremendously under priced and there is likely to be a bidding
war amongst several home buyers or renovators, we would never
consider offering more than 15% lower than the asking price. In
most cases, we start the bidding at a point that is more like 20% to
25% off the listing price. Remember, you are offering more than
money. You are offering a quick, painless, friendly transaction.
That counts. Our first few houses were purchased at an average of
79% of their asking prices. Those early negotiations taught us that
with a bit of intelligent negotiating we could make a tremendous
amount of money before we drove the first nail in the project.

Be prepared to negotiate after your initial offer and have a firm
strategy in mind. You should know what your absolute and final
maximum price is before you start negotiating. If your seller will
not budge, move on! There are plenty of other homes for you to
buy. Can you guess why people who sell things on E-bay love the
online auction format so much? It's because buyers get locked
on an item and will pay more than they should simply because
someone else wants it, too. Don't get sucked in.

Make a commitment at the start to never pay more than you should
for a property. Just as there is money to be made before you begin
working on your project, there is money to be lost as well. Do not

put yourself at a disadvantage at the start by paying more money than you should or more money than you need to.

When dealing with bank-owned properties, the rules change somewhat. As we mentioned elsewhere in this book, how and when banks make decisions on the offers they receive is a deep mystery. You should be prepared *not* to negotiate when dealing with a bank. It is possible that you will get a second chance to bid if your initial offer is too low, but it is unlikely. We have found it more likely that the bank will simply choose a higher offer if other offers have been made.

So do your homework and be sure that your initial offer is reasonable. You still have the advantages of speed and cash, even if the process is impersonal.

Should I Use a Home Inspector Prior to Purchase?

CHAPTER 13   **SHOULD I USE A HOME INSPECTOR
PRIOR TO PURCHASE?**

We could keep this chapter really short and simply say, YES!

But that would not be any fun. Let's consider why this is a good idea, shall we? If we had ever wondered if we were getting our money's worth from our inspector, Osburne Lane was all the assurance we needed.

Picture 5
Left: This waste line is wasted.

Picture 6
Right: One swift kick and this chimney could all end up in the basement.

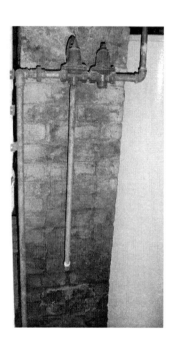

Osburne Lane was a home that Jim fell in love with. It was not in a great part of the city, but it was a great house. It had oak trim throughout, walk-up attic and an extra lot attached next door. And it was for sale for a very reasonable price! We could not miss. Or at least so we thought.

Jim was hooked and was ready to give the guy a deposit, while Craig firmly put the brakes on and insisted that we first have it inspected. When our friendly home inspector took a look, we were in for a nasty surprise. In our excitement (or, should we say, Jim's excitement), we had missed seeing asbestos in the basement, a serious drainage problem, an antique heating system, large holes in the main drain stack, and a deteriorating chimney squarely in the center of the house that threatened to collapse in on the roof at any moment.

These little items tripled the estimated cost of renovation. And of course we passed on this one. That $350 we paid our inspector was the best money we ever spent.

You want and need a home inspector who knows what you are trying to do and who will be honest with you. This is one of those cases where you would be very wise to develop a long-term relationship with someone you trust. You simply can not afford to be taken by surprise. We usually try to have our inspector look at the property before we make an offer, because anything we find to be substandard can then be brought to the seller's attention as reason for us to make a low offer.

Our inspector is a neutral party and his assessment of the property carries great weight in negotiations. He usually uncovers issues that the seller did not even know about. Those issues make it extremely easy to justify a lower offer and may even serve to make the seller grateful that someone wants to buy the house "as is."

Another benefit is that if there is a large issue that the inspector missed, his insurance company may be on the hook for his overlooking it. That could save you a ton of money.

And one last benefit, in most areas the local municipality requires the seller to obtain a certificate of occupancy before the sale unless the house is sold "as is." In that case, it is you who will need to get the C/O before you can sell it. And in most cases, your home inspector will not only uncover all of those little issues, he will usually do a more thorough job than the town's inspector. No nasty surprises at the end!

Do not scrimp on this one! Employing a home inspector is one of the very best moves you can make!

chapter **14**

Title Companies and Insurance

You may be tempted to eliminate one significant closing cost from your purchase price by not purchasing title insurance. We strongly advise against this! If you are buying properties in distress, the likelihood of there being tax liens or other judgments against a property is fairly high. If you purchase a property that has an unknown lien against it, you will almost certainly be sued. It has happened to us and thankfully we were covered.

If you do not have title insurance, you will need to fork over a pile of money to resolve an issue that you had nothing to do with. But if you have title insurance, you can simply smile and call your friendly title company. In a pleasant voice, tell them that your problem is now their problem, and you do not expect to hear any more about this issue, ever. What a nice feeling you will have!

Having property and liability insurance is also a great idea. As with any insurance, if your project is completed with no vandalism, theft or injury, you will wish you had not purchased protection. But it only takes one bad experience to convince you that the protection you are paying for is well worth the expense. You may have to shop around to find a company that will understand what you are doing and be able to meet your needs.

But we would strongly suggest that you establish a relationship with an insurance agent early on and figure those premiums into every project as a non-negotiable expense.

chapter 15

Deciding What Things to Renovate or Replace

A skill that you will need to develop quickly is the ability to walk into a house and make rapid and accurate decisions on what work needs to be done in order to make the maximum profit. This is an art, not a science. And you will probably make some mistakes at first. But knowing what needs to be repaired, removed, added or upgraded is one of the keys to making an accurate assessment of your eventual renovation costs.

Before you commit to purchase a home you will definitely want to hire a qualified home inspector to do a thorough engineering report and he will usually see things that you missed. But before you ask him to inspect the house, you need to know whether or not this project is one that will allow you to make a profit. And that means that you need to be able to walk in and in thirty minutes compose a list of things which need to be addressed.

Let's take a journey through an average house and assess each room and mechanical system to consider the level to which you will need to repair, replace or upgrade.

Exterior Issues

Roofs

One of the first things we look at when we visit a house that is for sale is the roof. It is relatively easy to spot trouble on a roof. Old, buckled, or missing shingles are a sure sign that trouble lies beneath. You would be surprised what havoc can be caused by even a small leak in a roof. And some of that havoc may not be immediately visible to you when you walk through the house. Damage may be hidden in walls, under eaves or in the attic.

This is not to say that we would never purchase a house with a faulty roof. We absolutely would. Sometimes the damage that a leaky roof causes can be an opportunity for us because it may result in superficial or cosmetic damage that keeps other people from being interested in buying the house. But remember that nobody buys a house to live in that has a bad roof, ever. You will need to repair or replace it if it is faulty or old.

Look for shingles that do not lie flat on the roof. If they are buckled this can be a sign that they are very old, or perhaps the attic has faulty ventilation and too much heat has been generated on the roof. Buckled shingles call for a new roof in almost every case. Missing shingles can signal leaks and are often a sign that the homeowner did not expend much time or money on basic maintenance.

Check the edges of the roof to see how many layers of shingles are visible. If you can see more than one layer, then you will need to budget for the total removal of both layers before a new roof may be installed. Look carefully for dips and bumps in the surface of the roof. These are signs that the plywood underneath the shingles is damaged. It may be rotten or delaminating, and in that case you will need to not only have the shingles replaced, but all of the damaged plywood as well. These kinds of repairs can add thousands of dollars to your renovation cost very quickly! Roofers do not work cheaply.

The bottom line concerning roofs is that you will almost certainly need to spend money to bring it to a state where the buyer has confidence that it will last for ten years. And many municipalities now require a special "roof certification" for any house being sold.

Gutters, Downspouts and Soffits

While you are looking at the roof, pay attention to the gutters. Effectively removing rain from a roof and diverting it to a location where it will not cause damage is more important than you might think. We once bought a house that had a wet, moldy basement. Walls had been damaged, the entire house smelled like old socks, and potential buyers were walking away in horror after visiting the basement.

Fortunately, we visited this house on a rainy day. And it was obvious to us that the trouble was not a leaky foundation, but one simple downspout that was draining water onto a concrete patio which was graded toward, rather than away from, the back of the house. It cost us $1.89 for a flexible downspout extension that we ran off the patio and onto a downgrade away from the house.

Within three weeks, the offending basement wall was bone dry. Check to see that the rain gutters are draining properly. This means that they should shed water onto a downgrade away from the house and should not terminate within three feet of the outside walls. An attractive plastic splash block may be a good, cheap solution for most drainage problems.

But where you do not see an appropriate place to terminate a gutter or in cases where the ground is not sloped away from the house you will need to plan on digging and laying plastic pipe to create some sort of underground system to move the water away from the foundation of the house. Home inspectors will notice bad drainage every time, so plan on fixing these problems from the start.

Gutters that are clogged, leaking, or do not have sufficient angle to move water to the downspouts represent a serious problem. Do not plan on ignoring rusty or leaking gutters.

If you have any question about the condition of the gutters on a house, plan on replacing them. Home Depot sells various plastic and metal systems for do-it-yourselfers, but these usually have joints every ten feet that are ugly and tend to leak.

Having a reputable contractor install an extruded, one-piece gutter will be well worth your while. And gutters, like roofs, are very visible and can add or subtract from the overall impression of your house when it is time to sell it.

The soffit is the flat part of the house that runs from under the roof edge back to the exterior wall. On many older houses the soffits are made of wood and since they get little sunlight and precious little ventilation in most attics they tend to not hold paint very well.

If you are having the roof and gutters installed, it would often be worth your investment to have the old wood soffits replaced with ventilated vinyl material that will never need to be painted. Buyers really like it when you throw around the term, "maintenance free!"

Chimneys

While you are looking at the roof, also be sure to notice the
condition of the chimney. This is a potentially expensive item to
repair if there are significant problems. Make sure that the chimney
has no obvious damage. If bricks are missing or it is leaning like
the Tower of Pisa, you will need to spend a pile of money.

It is not unusual to spend $12,000 to $20,000 if a chimney needs
to be totally rebuilt. If it has an outer coating of stucco or cement,
make sure that it is not deteriorating or cracking. Repairing the
outer covering may be somewhat inexpensive and may be done for
as little as $1,000.

If water has infiltrated this covering and the damage is extensive
beneath, you may need to do much more extensive and expensive
repairs. You will not be able to pass a final inspection in most
towns unless the chimney is sound and has proper flashing around
the roof.

Remember that most houses have some sort of combustion going
on inside. Even if the old fireplace is inactive, the chimney may
still be used by the gas or oil furnace or the hot water heater. We
have one friend, who, faced with a deteriorating chimney in the
center of his old house and a $20,000 estimate to fix it, decided
to simply remove it brick by brick. After all, none of the three
fireplaces in the house had been used in fifty years and each had
been effectively sealed and boarded over.

He had removed about ten feet of the chimney and had dropped it down below the roofline to a level just above the attic floor when, to his horror, he felt hot air coming up. He had forgotten that his gas furnace and gas hot water heater had been configured to vent into that old chimney. He ended up spending the $20,000 after all and his wife and friends have never missed a chance to ridicule him for his miscue.

Sidewalks, Patios and Driveways

Sidewalks and driveways are another very visible part of the exterior.

A fresh, new, concrete walkway is a high-impact item for your eventual buyer. Some municipalities will not even allow you to sell a home with crumbling or uneven concrete walkways. Of course,

Picture 7
Back porch of Cedar

Picture 8
Cedar—after

both concrete and asphalt may be patched for much less money than replacing them. But the message here is that you should not ignore these issues when you make your initial assessment of the house because they are likely to come back to haunt you later.

If we see bad concrete, we generally budget for a full replacement. We have often been able to patch it instead, but we would hate to be caught short on our estimate.

Landscaping

It is possible to spend tens of thousands of dollars on landscaping nearly any house. Landscaping is big business! But it is also a highly subjective business. This is obvious by the number of hideous concrete fountains and algae-choked goldfish ponds you will see in any neighborhood. Somebody thought that installing these were a good idea at some point, although we cannot imagine why.

But our point is that while it is possible to go overboard, it is also possible to ignore this high-visibility issue altogether. We plan on

Picture 9
The shed at Cedar did not look like much but it was solid as a rock structurally

Picture 10
New doors, a couple coats of paint and a new lawn make the difference

spending at least $1,500 on landscaping on every project that we do. Clearing brush, trimming or removing trees, planting some inexpensive bushes and flowers and putting down fresh mulch can transform a house.

For a small investment of time and money you can create a "wow factor" for prospective buyers, so always plan to spend at least a small amount of money on some reasonable landscape work. You may leave the fountains and goldfish ponds for the eventual buyer.

Paint and Trim

Unless the house has vinyl or aluminum siding that is in good condition, we always plan on spending money on painting the exterior of the house. A fresh coat of paint can do wonders for the look of a house and is almost always an investment that pays for itself later. Changing the color of the house to a pleasant, neutral color is a way to make a house blend in to its surroundings. Or, in a neighborhood where houses are older and in average or poor repair, a fresh coat of paint can make your house stand out. If the previous owner installed lavender siding, don't despair! That could represent an opportunity for you, not a problem. Some aluminum and vinyl siding can also be painted! Be sure to pay attention to the trim, soffits and fascia boards. All should be painted or capped with aluminum or vinyl. When you list your house for sale the buyer's first impression is important. A freshly painted exterior will be a signal to the buyer that you were serious about the renovation you have done.

Doors

The exterior doors make a statement, especially the front door. Nearly every home we have purchased has had an old, peeling door with bad weatherstripping. You would be surprised just how reasonable the price can be to replace an exterior door with a pre-hung door and frame. Modern doors have adequate weatherstripping and thresholds, and most have insulated cores as well. There is no need in most cases to budget for a top of the line door, but a reasonably priced fiberglass or metal door with nice top or side lights is a good investment.

Small Things

We are always careful to budget time and money for some little things that can make the exterior of a house look pleasing to the eye. We always replace the mailbox and the numbers on the house with new ones that match the style of the house. We also budget for a new doorbell and new storm doors where needed. These are relatively inexpensive, but are the things that people notice first when they walk in.

Interior Issues

Walls

Many old houses have interior walls that are in terrible condition. They may be old plaster walls that are cracked or deteriorating, they may be wallboard that has been damaged by people or water, they may be covered with old wallpaper that seems to have been glued on with epoxy, or they may have paneling that suggests an era that ended with bell-bottom jeans and neru collars.

Walls are not terribly expensive to deal with, but you must budget money to upgrade them if they are less than pristine. As a rule of thumb, we budget at least $1,000 in addition to the cost of our painter, for repairing and replacing walls. This would cover the cost of capping a few bad walls with ¼" sheetrock (a quick, easy fix) and replacing the walls in a bathroom or two. If we need to do more extensive work we usually figure on employing someone who can put up sheetrock and finish it. Depending on your relationship with the drywall contractor and the city where you live, you can probably count on paying between $0.50 and $0.75 per square foot ($25 to $36 per board) for sheetrock to be installed and finished, plus materials.

Larger jobs will cost far less per board since the contractor will not be interested in committing his crew for a job that is small. Installing and finishing drywall is an art and takes a professional only a fraction of the time it would take most amateurs to do the job. Our strong recommendation is that if you find yourself needing to cap or replace more than a room or two, have a pro do the job!

Be sure to figure on having every hole patched and every wall made smooth for painting. In nearly every case, leaving old paneling up is a bad idea. Old paneling looks outdated and cheap, even if it is painted a neutral color. But be prepared for a surprise when you remove it! That paneling may be hiding a gaping hole or some of that epoxy-glued wallpaper. It is rare to find a decent wall behind old paneling.

Trim

Trim is the kind of thing that can escalate your costs in a hurry. It is amazing how expensive trim can be. We generally try either to paint it or save what we can as we renovate rather than totally replacing it. But if you are capping lots of walls or totally renovating a kitchen or bath you will need to replace trim. That includes along the floors and around the doors and windows. Do not forget to account for this in your initial estimate.

Windows

If you are renovating older homes, you will become well acquainted with windows. Nearly every house we consider buying

Picture 11
60+ year old windows at Cedar

has broken, rotting, single-pane windows. You can definitely save some money by simply painting the old windows, but in most cases, scraping, re-glazing and painting old windows takes much longer than simply replacing them with modern double-pane replacement windows.

If you are paying someone to do this, you will not save much money over simply replacing them. We generally do replace the windows in older homes, feeling that the positive impression they make on energy-conscious buyers and the nice, fresh look they provide is well worth the money we will spend.

Replacement windows are a very high-markup item. In many places in the country if you have a contractor provide and replace them you may find yourself paying as much as $350 each.

Picture 1
p. 59
Holly—before

Picture 2
p. 60
Holly—after

Picture 3
p. 61

*Diamond in
the rough on
Osgood Lane?*

Picture 4
p. 62

*Beautiful
woodwork at
Osgood*

Picture 7
p. 109

Back porch of
Cedar

Picture 8
p. 110

Cedar—after

Picture 11
p. 116

60+ year old windows at Cedar

Picture 12
p. 117

New windows and flashing make for awesome curb appeal at Cedar

Picture 26
p. 161

Cedar—after

Picture 13
p. 118

Kitchen at
Ash—before

Picture 14, 15
pp. 119, 120

Kitchen at
Ash—after

Picture 16
p. 122

Cedar's kitchen— everything brand spanking new

Picture 17
p. 123

Kitchen at Ruggieri—after

Picture 18
p. 124

Kitchen at Holly—after

Picture 19
p. 127

*Bathroom at
Holly—after
(slightly nicer
neighborhood
gets tile)*

Picture 27
p. 173

*Bathroom at
Holly—after*

Picture 25
p. 142

*Beautiful floors
at Holly*

Picture 28
p. 174

Kitchen at
Holly—before

Picture 29
p. 175

Kitchen at
Holly—after

On the other hand, in most cities you may find good quality vinyl double-pane windows at Lowes or Home Depot for $125 to $175 and install them yourself. It is not a particularly hard job. If the windows are of a standard size, you will find replacement windows which can be fit and finished by an amateur in only twenty minutes each. It's a very simple procedure, one which window contractors don't want you to figure out for yourself.

If your home is older and has windows that are not of standard sizes, your replacement windows will need to be special ordered. We found a wholesaler on the internet who sold us all the windows we needed for one house, custom sized, for about $110 each. But then we chose to have a contractor install them for us for an additional $100 each.

Picture 12
New windows and flashing make for awesome curb appeal at Cedar

Despite the fact that the installation is easy, the thought of replacing 20-25 windows was going to cost us more time than we wanted to spend. As a rule of thumb, plan on replacing all of the old single-pane windows and budget at least $250 each.

Kitchens

It has been said that the kitchen sells the home. This is a wise saying. We make sure that in every house we renovate we pay special attention to the kitchen. It is the center of activity in most homes.

While you may easily spend tens of thousands of dollars upgrading a kitchen, we try to keep the scope of the project reasonable. But this is not an area where you can cut corners. Kitchens are subject

Picture 13
Kitchen at
Ash—before

to much scrutiny by prospective buyers, and most wives are a hard sell!

It must be said from the outset that the demographics determine the level of excellence in a kitchen. We do not put Corian countertops and Jennaire appliances in a $200,000 home. But if you do not figure on improving the kitchen to the standard of the neighborhood, you will have a very difficult time selling your house. Here are some of the component parts of a kitchen.

Cabinets

Cabinets need to be fresh, plentiful and strategically placed. In most renovation projects the old cabinets are the first thing to go. They are invariably beyond saving. In lower market homes you

Picture 14
Kitchen at
Ash—after

Picture 15
*Kitchen at
Ash—after*

may be able to upgrade the look of the cabinets by sanding and painting them.

But this is time-consuming. You can easily install "off-the-shelf" or unassembled cabinets for a very reasonable price and totally transform the kitchen. The idea is to make the kitchen look new and very functional.

At the risk of oversimplifying, cabinets tend to come in three basic grades. At the least expensive end you will find unassembled cabinets in standard sizes, made of particle board and coated with a synthetic covering. These may be colored or wood grain, but you will not find real wood anywhere. The hardware will be functional, but cheap.

We would not suggest using these for *any* renovation project, even low end projects. Cheap cabinets will deteriorate quickly and will not convey the message that you want to send to your prospective buyer.

The next step in quality is found in cabinets which are made of particle board, but have hardwood faces and doors. The sides will be covered with a synthetic covering, not real wood veneer. They may be unassembled or preassembled, but are still in standard sizes. The hardware is often of a better quality than the cheap cabinets.

These cabinets are sufficient for lower or mid range projects and may readily be found at Lowes, Home Depot or similar building supply stores. Although they are not built for the long haul, they are a reasonable alternative. You may find another short step upwards in quality with cabinets which have plywood bodies rather than particle board, but these will still be basic, inexpensive cabinets.

The highest priced cabinets will be made of hardwood, or at least plywood covered with high-quality hardwood veneer. They will have excellent hardwood faces and doors. They typically have top-quality hardware and may be ordered in custom sizes. The variety in colors, grains and finishes is endless. You will pay a premium for this type of cabinet.

For our purposes, working in mostly mid range homes, we have not ventured into this territory. But if you are working at the high

Picture 16
Cedar's
kitchen—
everything
brand spanking
new

end of the market, top quality cabinets will be something that the buyers will look for.

Be sure to install cabinets in every possible space. Buyers today are looking for storage. With a bit of experience you can easily figure a ball-park cost to replace cabinets in any kind of house, especially if you are using mid-quality cabinets in standard sizes.

Countertops

Like new cabinets, a brand new countertop makes an extremely positive statement.

Reasonably priced alternatives to granite or Corian abound, and for the money you will spend you will receive a good return. Be sure

Picture 17
*Kitchen at
Ruggieri—after*

to pick a neutral color! And do not forget to replace that kitchen sink and the faucet!

Appliances

In the scheme of things, appliances are not expensive. You can install a brand new stove and dishwasher of good quality for under $1,000. That is not a lot of money to spend in order to be able to show the buyer that he now has attractive appliances which will last for ten years.

If the house does not have a dishwasher, try very hard to integrate one into your plan. Dishwashers are an important selling point in most markets today. In one case we found that we did not have sufficient room for an installed dishwasher without sacrificing valuable lower cabinet space. Instead, we bought a roll-away

Picture 18
Kitchen at
Holly—after

dishwasher and left it, unused and in the original packing, in the kitchen.

Now, the buyer might have thought of buying one of these eventually. But for his wife to walk into the kitchen and see a dishwasher was well worth the $439 we spent!

We usually draw the line on refrigerators though. People's tastes vary on those. And they can be surprisingly expensive. We tend to leave that surprise for the buyer! But do plan to spend money on appliances if the ones in the kitchen are old or dated, are a color that does not match the room, or not as effective as they might be.

Lighting

It is amazing how effective lighting can transform a room. We always plan to add as much light as we can. We have found that an extremely effective and inexpensive option is to simply add a short track light on the ceiling above the sink.

For about $25 you will be able to throw light not only on the sink area, but also on the nearby countertops. Be sure to purchase a nice looking overhead light as well, and install the maximum wattage bulbs allowed. Lighting need not be an expensive proposition, but you do need to keep it on your list!

Floors

We will discuss floors later, but making the kitchen floor look new and pleasant is very important. You need not lay expensive tile in a lower or mid-range house, but be sure to budget for a good quality sheet vinyl floor, at least. If you are doing much of the renovation work yourself, installing this floor will be a breeze if you do it before you install the floor cabinets. The only time we have paid someone to install vinyl is when we have faced having to put in a seam. That seemed to be important enough to warrant having a professional do it!

To recap the kitchen discussion, it is hard to imagine buying a home for renovation and not spending at least $4,000 to $5,000 on the kitchen. Our average has been about $5,000, and that was with us doing most of the work ourselves because we really like renovating kitchens.

If the kitchen did not need that much help, the house would probably not be a renovation project! The trick is to quickly estimate the scope of the kitchen renovation. Be sure that you do not cut any corners on this room!

Bathrooms

Next to kitchens, bathrooms are the most important rooms in a house. You absolutely need the buyer to smile when he or she walks into the bathroom. And in many cases, that necessitates an extensive renovation. Like the kitchen, bathrooms have many component parts that may or may not need to be replaced or upgraded.

Vanities

People are looking for usable space and storage. We try to be sure that we maximize both the vanity top space and the storage space underneath. Replacing a tired, old vanity is a very inexpensive thing, so we almost always figure on doing this. A decent quality vanity, top and faucet can be purchased for less than $250 for a 36" system, even less for smaller bathrooms.

Toilets

Toilets are inexpensive to replace. For under $75 you can make the bathroom look fresh by changing out that old toilet. Don't go overboard on the fancy one-piece or trendy shaped toilets. Simply replacing the old unit with a good quality piece will be sufficient.

Picture 19
Bathroom at
Holly — after
(slightly nicer
neighborhood
gets tile)

Tubs and Showers

Replacing a tub or shower can be a more expensive and complicated proposition. For one thing, when you remove a tub or shower you will be exposing the plumbing. This complicates things right away and could be a reason to avoid doing violence to the tub or shower if they are not in terribly bad condition.

On the other hand, if a house has the original old tub or a moldy old shower enclosure you will most likely recoup your investment and more, besides adding that smile on your buyer's face.

Tile

A tiled bathroom makes a statement. But so does the bill you will receive from the installer. If you are handy and experienced working with tile and plan to do your own work, tiling the bathroom walls, at least behind the tub, may make good sense.

In a lower end house there are many less expensive alternatives. But in a mid range house, people are looking for tile, not plastic tub or shower enclosures. We would recommend finding a reliable and reasonably priced contractor who can install inexpensive tile for you.

Ventilation

It is surprising how many bathrooms in older homes do not have adequate ventilation. In today's homes the building code usually proscribes ventilating fans. If you have easy access to the space above the bathroom it is a relatively simple and inexpensive thing to install an overhead fan. Adding a second electrical wire to allow you to control the fan and overhead light separately from a single location is a great idea as well and may be done easily during renovation.

Floors

Despite what you may hear about self-stick vinyl tiles being much better today than a generation ago, they are still a poor alternative to a one-piece vinyl or tile floor. We almost always plan to upgrade the bathroom floor, but pay attention to your market.

In anything other than high-end homes, a one-piece sheet floor is usually a sufficient upgrade and takes a fraction of the time to install. But if you are having tile installed around the tub or

Picture 20
Basement of
Cedar—after

shower, it might be a good idea to install a tile floor as well. This will add some expense, but it will add value as well.

Basements

Creating usable space out of unused space is like adding square feet to a home. One place where you may find potential space is the basement. Since we usually renovate homes that are older, we tend to find that most unfinished basements have deteriorated the point where it takes some vision to reclaim their potential. Here are some tips that can help you to maximize the space you have and impress your potential buyers.

First, plan on painting everything. By "everything" we mean painting the floor, walls, and even the ceiling joists if there is no sheetrock covering them. A coat of white paint on the walls and

Picture 21
Basement of
Holly—after

ceiling can transform a dingy, dark basement into an inviting space for storage, a workshop, or a laundry. Be sure to paint the cement floor with a durable floor paint.

Most municipalities have strict codes that govern what can be called a below-ground bedroom or living space. The ceiling height, the presence of windows and the number of emergency egress routes usually determines how you may characterize basement space. Even if you cannot advertise that your house has a basement family room or an extra subterranean bedroom, by painting and sprucing up the space just enough to suggest its potential you can make your point without running afoul of the building inspector.

Picture 22
Hide that unsightly water main

Creating simple shelving or fashioning small closets and storage areas can be done for pennies, but will make a big impact on buyers who are looking for space to store their stuff.

Of course, if your house already has a finished basement, that is a bonus for your buyer. Be sure that by the time you sell the home all moisture issues are fully addressed. You need to create a space that is so inviting that people are pleasantly surprised when they walk down the stairs.

We always take a flashlight and carefully inspect the perimeter of the basement, looking for leaks or evidence that water has infiltrated walls, floor or foundation. Inspecting the house on a rainy day is a good idea!

A wet or leaking basement is not only unpleasant; it may even constitute a health hazard if it aids the growth of mold. Wet basements also draw termites and can rot wood and concrete block, creating structural hazards.

If the basement leaks, fixing the problem may be as simple as redirecting a downspout to divert runoff from the gutters more effectively, or grading the dirt along the foundation walls to shed water. But some leaky basements need extensive and expensive remediation. Be sure that you make a thorough inspection and then have your professional inspector evaluate it as well!

Attics

When you inspect the attic in your home be sure to check for signs of water damage, rodents, or other animals who may have taken up residence. We often find evidence of a roof having leaked at some point and we simply make sure that the leaking is not an active problem. Evidence of rodents, birds or animals suggests that these pests are infiltrating the house from the outside and care must be taken to find out the source of their entry.

The majority of the heat loss in a house is through the attic. Proper insulation solves this problem effectively. Likewise, adequate insulation can also cut cooling bills significantly. Insulating an attic is a relatively inexpensive proposition and is a great selling feature, so we usually budget to upgrade the insulation if it is inadequate.

Be sure to notice the ventilation in the attic as well. If there is not ventilation along the ridge line, in the eaves, or in the soffits, you may need to address that issue. By simply adding some boards on the floor you can create extra storage space; so if the attic is relatively easy to access you might consider doing this.

Every once in a while we find a home that warrants consideration of the attic as livable space. Before you get too excited about this prospect, be sure to note that in most cases you will need to add heating ducts or pipes and this can be a fairly expensive proposition.

You will also likely need to add insulation, ventilation (additional or larger windows?), staircases and handrails consistent with building codes, sheetrock, electrical outlets and fixtures, paint and carpet. While this may possibly be a worthy investment, control your enthusiasm for reclaiming this unused space until you get an accurate estimate of what it will cost!

As we suggested with basements, sometimes the best thing to do is only enough work to suggest the *potential* of the space to your buyer rather than finishing the work. Your buyer has the option to obtain a permit and get inspections or not, and may choose whether or not to conform to every line of the building code. You do not have that option!

Heating and Air Conditioning

Buyers today are looking for fuel-efficient and reliable heating systems in their homes. Most homes we purchase have very old

Picture 23
New HVAC is a great help in selling a home

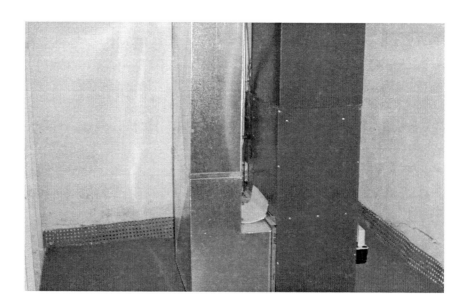

heating plants, so we typically plan to spend money replacing the furnace or boiler. Although you might need to invest $3,000 - $5,000, we believe that the money will be well spent. Husbands typically look at the heating system as critically as wives look at kitchens. Being able to advertise the fact that you have installed a brand new heating system will be a huge selling point.

If the home has an older central air conditioning unit, if it is functional you probably will not need to replace this. But we do look for an opportunity to upgrade the whole system if possible. If a home already has a forced air heating system, it is not terribly expensive to add a central air conditioning unit. Again, in most areas of the country this will be a major selling point.

We once bought a property that had electric baseboard heat. Electric heat is absolutely the least efficient heating system you can have. We debated it for a while, but decided that we simply would not be able to get a decent price, or even much buying traffic, with such an antiquated system. Since this was a one floor ranch-style house with easy access to the floors from the basement, we reasoned that the ducting would be relatively easy to do.

And we were pleasantly surprised that the gas company agreed to run a gas line from the street to the house for free. We ended up tearing out every electric baseboard and contracting a HVAC specialist to install ductwork, a brand new high-efficiency gas heater and central air.

Although we spent nearly $10,000 on this upgrade, we firmly believe that we received every penny back, and more, when we

sold the house. You may not need to do such radical surgery, but
it is worth considering how you might upgrade the heating and air
conditioning systems in a home.

Hot Water Heaters

The hot water heaters in most older homes have seen at least ten
years of service. Even the best heaters are only guaranteed for
eight to ten years, and most inexpensive units are not built to last
nearly that long. Replacing a hot water heater is a relatively simple
thing in most houses, and a decent unit can almost always be
bought for under $400.

We consider this a sound investment and a great selling point. It
buys peace of mind for your new owner, who would otherwise be
wondering if he may wake up without hot water or find a flooded
basement. With a ten year old water heater, both are distinct
possibilities!

Electrical Systems

When inspecting your house prior to purchase, be sure to note the
condition of the electrical system. When most older homes were
built the total anticipated drain on the electrical system was a
fraction of today's demands. Think about it. A 60 year old home,
while still quite attractive and serviceable in most respects, was
simply not wired to cope with multiple computers, plasma TV's,
blow-dryers, curling irons, dishwashers, garbage disposals, trash
compactors, microwave ovens, food processors, air conditioners
and power shop tools. If we see a house with old, glass, "spin-

Picture 24
Electric upgrade at Ruggieri

in" fuses, we know that we are looking at a major expense for an electrical upgrade.

Those old fuse panels simply will not handle the load today and may be a safety hazard. In a small modern house the bare minimum amperage is 100 amps. More typical for a newer or larger house is 150 or even 200 amp service. But we have looked at many houses that have only a 60 amp service panel, even if they did have modern circuit breakers rather than the old glass fuses.

Besides checking the adequacy of the service panel, be sure to inspect the wiring. Inadequate or faulty wiring is a fire and safety hazard. Although adding a circuit breaker to an existing and adequate service panel is a cheap and simple thing, doing major upgrading to the electrical system in a house is quite expensive indeed.

Some old homes have "post and tube" wiring, which is both obsolete and dangerous. Although some building codes will "grandfather" these old systems and not require a total replacement, we would not sleep well if we sold a home with such inadequate wiring to a modern-day buyer.

Of course, your home inspector will be able to give you a much better assessment later, but in the initial walk through you will want to note how old and adequate the system is and whether or not the wiring appears to be in good condition. Just because an old line is fused with a new 20-amp circuit breaker, that does not guarantee that the wire is adequate to handle a 20-amp load.

In many older homes the grounding of outlets and switches is also inadequate. In virtually every old home we have purchased, we have found at least one burned out switch or outlet that crackles, smokes or sparks when you use it. These are dangerous! We plan on changing virtually every outlet and switch in the house and ensuring that they are adequately grounded. This is a quick and inexpensive job, but one that you need to put on your list.

Plumbing

A plumber was called to a doctor's home to do some work. After working for twenty minutes, the plumber gave the M.D. a bill for $300. The doctor said, "Good gracious! I have been to medical school and residency and have been practicing medicine for over

20 years and I can't charge that kind of money!" The plumber smiled and said, "Yeah, I couldn't either when I was in medical practice."

You have probably heard that old joke before, but when we see a house with plumbing issues, we draw a deep breath. A leaky sink or a bad toilet gasket is a small thing, but improper venting, a cracked drain pipe, or galvanized water supply lines are a serious matter.

We once inspected a house in which the entire water supply was tied together from the rusting well-pump to the kitchen and bath with two-foot sections of PVC pipe, each with a Home Depot sticker still on it and joined to the next section with what looked like super glue. It is amazing how bad the plumbing can be in some older homes.

And what is even more amazing is how much it can cost to make it right. We usually defer to our professional home inspector on plumbing issues. He has often identified issues that we never would have seen or suspected in our initial walk through. But let us list a few things you should look for as you make your own initial inspection.

Notice what kind of material the water pipes are made of. You will not find much PVC (white, plastic pipe) in old homes, but you will generally see either copper or galvanized iron. Copper is good; iron is bad. This is because iron rusts. And as it rusts it creates potentially catastrophic problems. The following citation is taken from the AmeriSpec home inspection service:

Galvanized supply and distribution piping was historically installed in homes prior to 1950. These pipes commonly rust or corrode from the inside out, often reducing the pressure or restricting the flow of water or worse yet, leaking and creating flood damage to a home.

Life expectancies for galvanized plumbing are generally on the order of 40-50 years. Given that many galvanized pipe installations have recently reached their estimated life expectancies, the risk of a pipe leak occurring and the potential for flood damage is high. Some insurance companies are now refusing to provide homeowner's insurance on houses with this type of plumbing, particularly for new policies.

http://www.amerispec.ca/english/brochures/plumbing.htm

If you see galvanized or iron pipes, you are usually looking at trouble. This does not mean that every pipe must be replaced—you may perhaps leave that for the buyer to do at some later time, especially if the piping seems to currently be in good repair. But even if it appears to be in good condition, the inside of the pipe may be severely rusted and that rust can restrict the flow of water. Galvanized pipe is a problem waiting to happen and its presence will have a bearing on how much you can expect to receive for the house when you sell it.

Look very hard for signs of leaks. Check ceilings, floors, Even if the leaks happened a very long time ago, the repairs may not have been adequate and they may also signal a larger and unaddressed issue. Another thing to remember is that where a valve or pipe has leaked for a long time there is likely to be rot and deterioration of the wood in the area. This means having to do carpentry in addition to plumbing!

The drainage system in the house is incredibly important. Old cast iron drain lines can spring leaks and necessitate replacing long runs of pipe. Check thoroughly in the basement or crawlspace and make note of any little "stalactites" that appear to be hanging from cast iron pipes. They tend to signal tiny pin-holes that are caused by rust. Your professional inspector will be able to spot trouble for you, but in that initial inspection before you decide to make an offer on the house, you do need to get a clear picture of what kind of plumbing repairs you will need to make.

Insulation

In 1950, the cost of a barrel of oil was $1.71. In 2005, the price topped out at over $60 per barrel. How many home builders do you think gave thought to the cost of heating a home in 1950? Very few! With heating oil and natural gas costing a tiny fraction of today's prices, insulating a home was largely unnecessary. You will find that many old homes do not have insulation at all, and those that do often have inadequate insulation.

Today's buyer is educated about the cost of heating a home. And your buyer knows that an uninsulated home is going to cost a small fortune to heat and cool. This is not to say that we spend money to contract a professional to add insulation to every old home that we renovate. But anytime we open an exterior wall we are careful

Picture 25
*Beautiful floors
at Holly*

to add an appropriate amount of insulation before we close it
up. The attic is the place where the majority of heat is lost in the

winter, and it is where the greatest infiltration of heat occurs during the summer months. For that reason, you would be wise to add insulation to the attic as a selling point if you are easily able to do so.

Floors

We plan to spend a significant amount of money upgrading the floors in most homes that we renovate. There are two reasons for this. First, the floors make an immediate statement to the buyer. If she walks in and sees gleaming new vinyl or tile in the kitchen and bathrooms, polished hardwood floors in the living room and brand new carpet in the bedrooms, she will smile.

And we really like it when buyers smile. Your realtor does, too. The second reason you should plan on upgrading most floors is that buyers do not wish to spend any more money or time completing your renovation. They generally want to move in the very day they close the transaction.

Moreover, they do not have the money or the time to spend refinishing floors or replacing carpet. Even if the floors are not badly worn all over the house, the buyer knows that at some point she will need to remove every bit of her furniture from the offending rooms in order to have the floors dealt with. And this will not make her smile.

In most cases, the cost of refinishing hardwood floors and the cost of installing mid-grade carpet is roughly the same. Our choice depends on the condition of the floors and also on the market in which the house is located. In lower end neighborhoods, carpet is best. In higher end neighborhoods, we tend to refinish hardwood floors if the house has them. It is a fairly simple thing for you to get a ball-park estimate per square foot for each of these in your particular market. This will effectively inform your budget as you evaluate the house.

As we mentioned earlier, in bathrooms we tend to use one-piece vinyl flooring. Tile is a nice option, but it is pricey. The same is true for kitchens. But in every case we make sure that the floors are attractive, neutral in color and of decent quality.

Recap

After reading this chapter you may be feeling a bit overwhelmed. You probably had never thought about the fact that there are so many component parts in a home! As you can see, the list of items that may need to be replaced, repaired or upgraded is enormous. On our first few projects we tended to overlook many of these things because we were anxious to get moving and just a bit overly optimistic about the condition of the homes we bought. Although we were wise enough to have built in a significant cushion (the Cunningham Factor) and still made money, we are now glad that we have the experience to anticipate the majority of the potential expenses that we will incur. This has contributed significantly to our own peace of mind, and ultimately, to our profit margin.

You will do well to study this list to the point where it will become second nature to make an accurate assessment when you visit a potential project. When we walk through a house before making an offer, we often sit in the car and come up with a ball-park figure on what our renovation costs may be. Then, later, we use a detailed spreadsheet to make a more accurate assessment before making a decision. Even after our first three projects, it was amazing to see how close our ball-park figures, calculated on a napkin in the front seat, had begun to come to our final numbers, done on a spreadsheet. You will develop a feel for this game fairly quickly, so don't despair!

chapter 16

Repairs Estimate
Checklist

Knowing what it will cost to renovate your project before you purchase it is incredibly important, because therein lays your ability to estimate your potential profit or loss. But arriving at an accurate estimate is nearly impossible because you simply cannot control so many of the variables involved. Will you discover hidden damage? Will the cost of materials or labor increase? (At this writing, some prognosticators within the building industry are projecting enormous price increases for lumber and sheetrock due to the massive amounts of these materials which will be needed to reconstruct the Gulf Coast after hurricanes Katrina and Rita in 2005.) Have you simply overlooked something? Will you damage something during renovation? (Jim once severed a Freon line with a drill, nicked a hidden water pipe with a nail, and another time punctured a natural gas line with a reciprocating saw. Can you see why we included this concern in the list?) Materials may be damaged, stolen or mistakenly cut too short to be used ("Craig, where did we put that 'board stretcher?'").

We know that if we had arrived on a fool-proof system at the start, we would have saved ourselves a significant amount of anxiety. But we forged ahead with the little expertise we had, estimating generously, and hoping that we would not get burned too badly when our projections became real dollars spent. Therefore, we feel that it would be helpful for you if we provide a list which will help you to quickly figure out how much your own renovation will cost. The trouble is, this list, written in New Jersey late in 2005, is subject to its own regional economics and cannot account for inflation or price increases. Still, we don't figure that there are too many markets around the country where things cost more than the New York metropolitan area! So it is possible that this list will be useful in Little Rock, and it may continue to be useful for a while longer in economies which are not as inflated as the New York metro area. With all of these caveats and disclaimers in mind, here is a very rough idea of how you might estimate the renovation of a typical three bedroom, two bath house in a lower middle class neighborhood. Our spreadsheet, found elsewhere in the book, allows us to plug in the estimates for the component parts, including purchase, sales and holding costs. But for the sake of argument, here is a sample list of repairs and upgrades and some estimated costs.

Exterior

Roof: 0 - $8,000, depending on condition.
It is relatively easy to get a price per square foot from several contractors and come up with an average cost. This will vary depending on three basic scenarios. If the plywood underneath the shingles is good and there is only one layer of shingles, you can simply add another layer. This is not expensive. If the roof already has two layers of shingles, the roof must be torn off before a new layer can be added. This is more expensive. Finally, if the plywood is damaged, the entire covering may need to be removed right down to the joists. This is much more expensive.

Gutters: 0 - $1,500.
We usually budget about $1,000 if the home needs new gutters.

Chimney: 0 - $15,000.
Pray that you do not need extensive work! To simply replace the

stucco coating on a small chimney or to repoint a few bricks may only cost $750. To rebuild a chimney is a major expense.

Masonry Work: 0 - $3,000.
Most homes only need some patching done to the sidewalks, masonry steps and driveway. But some building codes will not grant a certificate of occupancy without these items being rehabilitated. We usually budget $500 - $1,000 if it does not look like we will need any extensive work done.

Landscaping: $500 - $2,000.
Of course you may budget much more than this, but we figure on spending a minimum of $500 on yard clean up, plantings, mulch. If you need a retaining wall or more significant landscaping, you will need to revise your estimate upwards.

Paint and trim: $2,500 - $5,000.
We have found a reliable painter who will do an average house, inside and out, for about $3,500. We budget this on nearly every job we do. It is important to make the home look fresh and new, both inside and out.

Exterior doors: $500 - $1,000 if we need a new door.

Small exterior things: $500.
This covers a doorbell, mailbox, welcome mat, house numbers, etc.

Interior

Walls: $750 - $3,500.
This estimate depends on whether we can patch most of the walls and replace only a few, or if we need to do extensive sheet rock replacement.

Trim and doors: $1,000.
Replacing old interior doors with fresh, colonial doors will cost you about $75 each. We avoid replacing massive amounts of trim, but where it is needed, it can be expensive.

Windows: $2,500 - $3,500.
The window companies that deposit flyers on your car at the supermarket or advertise via mass-mailings will charge much more, but we usually can replace every window for less than $200 each if we shop around or do the work ourselves.

Heating: 0 - $4,000.
For most homes we plan on spending approximately $3000 to replace the heating system. If the heater is old, this will be an investment that will get a good return when you sell the home.

Air conditioning: 0 - $4,000.
If a home has a serviceable central air conditioner, we usually do not replace it. If the home has none and one can be added easily, we usually plan on doing that. This is another significant investment that will pay off when you sell the house because many buyers in warmer climates will simply exclude homes from their search if they do not have central air.

Kitchen: $2,000 - $6,000.

High quality materials can double this estimate, but with most small kitchens we can totally renovate it, including appliances, for about $5,000. If you have someone else do the work, you may need to significantly increase this estimate.

Bathrooms: $1,000 - $7,000.

We budget about $500 per bathroom to "freshen it up" with a new vanity and toilet. We budget about $2,500 per bathroom for a total renovation. And we budget about $3,500 per bathroom if we are having someone else do the work.

Electrical: $300 - $5,000.

At minimum, you will want to replace all of the switches and outlets in an older home, as well as many lighting fixtures. A new electrical panel will likely run you about $2,000 or more. If you need more wiring, you can easily double that estimate.

Plumbing: $500 - $10,000.

You will be replacing sinks and faucets in nearly every home you renovate. These may all be done for less than $500. Pray that you do not run into larger issues!

Floor coverings: $2,000 - $5,000.

As we suggested elsewhere in this book, it is a simple thing to get estimates per square foot for installing a mid-grade carpet or refinishing hardwood floors. We typically budget $3,500 for the whole house if is of average size.

Paint: This estimate was covered in the painting estimate for the exterior. It makes sense to have the same painter do the whole job.

Little things: $300 - $500.
We plan on replacing every door hinge if they are old and dirty. We also replace every door handle. Some interior window hardware should be replaced. You can spend $500 or more very quickly on small things like this.

chapter **17**

Inspections and
Permits

One reason why many homeowners do not do much work on their own homes is because they assume that a permit is needed for most every job and improvement. This is just not the case. In fact, many municipalities give homeowners great latitude and are easy to work with. On the other hand, there are instances when the whole permitting process can be daunting indeed.

In general — get permits. They are not very difficult to obtain and a nosy neighbor could make a mess of your whole renovation if they report you for doing work without permits. Moreover, you may be asked by a prospective buyer whether or not some of the more extensive renovation was done with permits and inspections. You will not want to answer that question in the negative!

When Inspections and Permits are Needed

The words "renovate," "repair" and "remodel" are all fairly subjective. As we stated in an earlier chapter, we have generally tried to stay away from major remodeling projects that include adding space or changing structural characteristics of a home.

When you make significant structural changes you are necessarily looking at a plethora of permits and inspections. As long as you are using licensed contractors, this may not pose much of a problem for you. But it can add time and expense and invite unwanted scrutiny of the entire renovation.

It would be a good idea to make a trip down to the local municipality's construction office. If you approach the folks who work there in a friendly way and with a genuine cooperative spirit, they are usually quite accommodating. Remember their perspective. They have been charged with the responsibility of ensuring that homes are safe. That is a noble trust.

The problem comes when a few of them decide that they have pretty much unlimited power to stymie the efforts of homeowners and honest contractors and make the inspection and permitting process into their own little fiefdom. You can usually tell the difference pretty quickly between a conscientious inspector and one of these inspector-zealots.

But in either case, it will generally do you much more good to be friendly and cooperative than to be defensive and testy. You might ask for a publication that lists exactly what kinds of work requires a permit in your town. This varies from place to place.

Inspectors are looking for things that make homes unsafe. And if you are renovating older homes, there are probably things like that in your home. Most municipalities do not require that every system be brought up "to code" and can extend grace where some existing systems may be somewhat substandard.

But it is both unwise and immoral to try to hide unsafe wiring, rotted wood or leaky plumbing when you know it is there. Having said that, not every substandard system is actually unsafe. For instance, some old wiring may be perfectly acceptable to keep around so long as proper grounding is done.

Here is our strategy for dealing with local inspectors. First, if your property has failed the initial inspection for occupancy (likely if you are buying "as is"), be sure to make each and every repair in an excellent manner. This will suggest to your local inspector that you are acting in good faith. You might even have an unnecessary conversation with him to ask a few questions about the list. This will also demonstrate your intention to act in good faith.

In those cases where you may be doing mostly cosmetic work and will not be needing permits, it is wise not to attract a lot of attention to your project by having trade vans and trucks around the property on a regular basis, or having a 30 cubic yard dumpster in your front yard.

These things tend to be signals that you are undertaking a large project. Though you may have nothing to hide or fear, it is not fun to have an inspector visiting you regularly to make sure that you are not doing significant structural or technical work. For this reason we try to minimize the visibility of both trade vans and dumpsters.

chapter 18

How to Choose Contractors

You will almost certainly need at some point to hire a contractor, or perhaps many contractors, to complete a renovation. In fact, we have found that we were better served to hire a contractor to do much of the work that we could do ourselves.

There are simply many things that can be done much more rapidly and with better quality by a professional. You will begin to figure out which things these are based on your own abilities and the things that you do and don't like to do.

Some things are a function of expertise. We have found that it is best to hire folks to do things on either extreme of the expertise scale. "Grunt work" that requires absolutely no talent (clearing brush, cleaning out the basement, some demolition work) or more technical things like plumbing and complicated electrical work are things that we look for people to do for us.

Other things may fall in the middle of the technical scale, but people with experience and a large crew or quality tools can make short work of these projects and save you precious time.

Examples of these things would be installing windows (after you buy them yourself to save the exorbitant mark-up that a contractor will add!), doing roofing and installing gutters. Each of those examples are things that we could easily do ourselves, but it would take us many times the amount of time that professionals can do it in. For example, one of the houses we renovated needed 23 windows.

Picture 26
Cedar—after

We could have saved $100 per window if we had installed and flashed the windows ourselves. It took a pro about one day to install the windows but four days for him to put flashing around them. For us, that job would have taken weeks, not to mention the fact that the flashing would have looked terrible. Installing flashing is an art, and we are not artists, yet.

Choosing contractors is another art form. On the low end, you may find that college and high school kids and local laborers may be employed quite inexpensively. On the higher and technical end, you will quickly find yourself with many choices. How do you decide which contractor to choose?

First, be sure to seek several estimates. This is common wisdom, and contractors are quite aware that this is the game that smart homeowners will employ. They tend to fight back by doing a couple of things. First, they may under-estimate the cost of the project, hoping to gain back some money after they are engaged by finding extra "problems." Or they may add on hidden costs like charging you $20/hour to run to the hardware store.

You will need to be sure that you outline all of the possible scenarios to protect yourself against this kind of thing. Of course, the contractor is entitled to extra compensation if the scope of the project changes in mid-stream. But that is not the issue here.

The issue is making sure that you and your prospective contractor agree on any potential costs over and above your original contract. Simply asking the contractor, "this is for EVERYTHING, right?" several times at the end of your negotiation goes a long way to keeping extra costs down.

How do you get estimates? Well, you will need to have a list of contractors. The yellow pages are an obvious source of names, as are newspapers and referrals from people you know. There are advantages to calling large companies and advantages to calling small companies. We usually call both.

Large companies can often work quickly and may save you time and possibly money by working in volume. They are easy to find in the phonebook, they have experience, manpower and they often have a good reputation in a community with building inspectors.

But the large company's overhead is greater than that of the small company. They often don't really need your business, will not do small jobs and will sometimes charge higher prices than small companies. We have found that the companies with the huge ads in the yellow pages tend to charge the highest prices because they have the most visibility and the most overhead.

Sometimes a great deal may be found by engaging a smaller company. Smaller companies tend to advertise in newspapers, and we have found some good deals and good contractors by looking for "handyman" or "full service" guys who can handle a variety of trades.

Once in a while you will find in the newspapers a retired guy who is not working so much for the money as he is to stay busy and make a few bucks on the side. This kind of person can be a real help and may be someone whose phone number you want to keep handy!

The small company or handyman may not be able to begin work on your project immediately, but in other cases they are starved for work, having lost potential customers to the big companies in the area. As owners of a very small company, we do tend to favor the "Mom and Pop" companies just out of empathy.

But you would be wise to do your homework before making a decision. Do they have their own equipment? Are they insured? Do they have a good reputation and can they provide you with references?

Another way to find potential contractors is to ask the ones who are currently working for you who it is that they would recommend in other trades. They will absolutely have other names for you. And assuming that you are pleased with the one you hired initially and intend to continue to do business with him, engaging his friends may make for a great relationship where contractors doing various trades will cooperate with one another on the site.

This method of finding contractors is naturally self-correcting. For instance, our heating contractor knows what we like and what we value in a contractor (quality, price, speed) and will not refer us to an electrician that is expensive and slow. Having a good relationship with your contractors is essential. If you do not have a good relationship with one in a particular trade, find another and another on your subsequent jobs until you find one with whom you work well.

As you compile estimates, make it plain that this is what you are doing. There is no use in being less than honest about the process. This is business, and the contractors understand that. But have the courtesy to call each one back and let them know that you have decided to go with another estimate. You might want to do this before you actually let your first choice know that he has the job. That way you remain open to a quick price reduction from a contractor who really wants the job.

We do not always choose the lowest bid. There is more at stake here than money. In some areas the reputation of the contractor will really help you in the inspection process, and the fact that a contractor is licensed makes a difference if you are pulling permits for a job. Speed and quality also count and might be reasons to choose a contractor who charges a bit more than some others.

There is another way to receive good prices from contractors. Let them know that you are aware of the fact that working on a vacant home is much more attractive to contractors than working on an occupied home. Think of the hassles that contractors avoid by working on a vacant property! Children, limited working hours (no weekends, early mornings or evenings), dogs, cats and worrying about keeping the house clean—all of these things are avoided by working with you! You offer the contractor much more flexibility and ease of access. Use this awareness to negotiate a better price.

Scheduling will be important to you and to your contractors. Contractors are running a business. One of their most important goals is to have all of their employees working on jobs five days a week. If they miss a day in a given week because of a scheduling conflict or lack of business they are out 1/5 of the possible revenue for that week. And they still have to pay their people. Multiply that by a year and imagine how that could hurt their bottom line.

Your renovation project could be a fantastic solution for these guys. Here's how. Your heating contractor takes on your job and you tell him that he can spread the work out over as long as a month. Money signs are dancing in his head because he now knows that it is very unlikely that he will have any days this month when his people are not working. You have saved this contractor a significant amount of money by being flexible. Some of this money can be passed on to you in the form of a lower bid, if you are shrewd enough to point this out to him.

Remember to give your contractors a key to the property if you trust them. This will help them be flexible and meet their goals.

The most important thing to remember is that you are doing more than solving a plumbing or electrical problem here. You are looking for a relationship. Yes, you will be doing this for a while and you want to develop a cadre of contractors whom you trust and who will work for you fairly, honesty and quickly.

It would be wise to state that up front in the bidding process... let them know that you are not merely looking for one job to be done, but potentially dozens of jobs over the years to come. That might help you a bit as you negotiate that first deal.

chapter 19

How to Deal With Contractors

As we suggested in an earlier chapter, we have always maintained, as a core value, that we are doing more than renovating houses or making money. We are building relationships. That means that we always treat our contractors as more than functionaries. We treat them with dignity, respect, and courtesy. This is primarily because we believe that this is the way that people deserve to be treated.

But it also has its benefits to our business. It tends to ensure that our contractors will do quality work, give an honest effort, and be available to us again at a fair price. Some of that dynamic is created in the way we interact with them verbally. But there are little things you can do, as well, that really help develop your relationship.

How about providing cold beverages on a hot day? Or lending a hand in an odd moment. Asking them what radio station they would prefer to listen to. Paying them on time and in full immediately upon completion of the project. We once bought a crew of sheetrock guys a 12-pack of their favorite beer and gave it to them just before they left the site one Friday afternoon.

You get the idea. It's a relationship, not merely a contract. And if you treat it as such, you will reap benefits in the end. Besides, it's the right thing to do! Don't you want to be treated as more than a drone?

But even though you are developing a relationship, this is still business. For that reason we try not to pay more than 25% up front. We try to simply pay for materials up front, not labor. Or, if the project takes a long time, we will advance up to 50% of the total to help cover the crew's labor. But it is always a good idea to withhold as much as you can until you are totally satisfied with the job.

If you discover problems after the job is supposed to be finished, it is next to impossible to gain the attention of a contractor who is paid in full! But when they are done, really done, be sure to pay them immediately. After they get over the shock of not having to bill you several times, they will be ingratiated to you for life. We cannot understand how some businesspeople sleep at night when they have "borrowed" funds from contractors at 0% interest by not paying them for 30 days or more after completion of the job. That's just wrong.

One last piece of advice we can give you is this: learn to speak their language. Like anyone, contractors are usually glad to tell you what they are doing, where they learned their trade, and how they do what they do. Asking lots of questions will help you to understand the nature of that trade, and this will be a significant advantage for you when you move on to your next renovation project.

The idea here is not so much to learn how to do the job and, thereby, exclude a contractor next time; although that is not a terrible idea. The real goal is to educate yourself so that you can keep the upper hand in negotiations, and so that as you assess potential properties you have a good understanding of what needs to be done and how much it will cost to do it. Pay attention to everything!

chapter 20

Why They Will Buy
Your Home

The process of getting folks to choose your home over others on the market is actually quite easy. There are lots of books and publications out there which detail the things that buyers are looking for, but actually it is a pretty simple science.

The first thing to keep in mind is that the vast majority of buyers are extending themselves to buy a home in the first place. They are generally looking at or near the top of the market in which they qualify for a mortgage. If they have $15,000 available for a down payment and closing costs and they can afford to spend $1,500/month on principle, interest and taxes and that will buy them a $250,000 home, then they are generally looking for a $250,000 home. You might think it would be wise for them to look instead for a $225,000 home and have some money and credit left over to do improvements, but that is usually not the case.

People tend to want to buy as much house as they possibly can. What that means is that the buyer is not looking seriously at a home in need of new wall-to-wall carpet, a kitchen renovation or massive landscaping. Most buyers walk into a home with bad (or no) carpet and see an $8,000 expense. If they shopped around and negotiated with carpet dealers, they might find that it would cost half that much to re-carpet the entire house. But their first impression will be an expensive impression.

So the message here is this: take care of the basic needs and take care of them well! That 40 year old heater? The buyer is thinking that this will cost him $10,000 this year even though your inspector thinks it might last for five more years. Spend the $5,000 and replace it! It will add a sense of peace of mind to your buyer. And

Picture 27
Bathroom at
Holly—after

Picture 28
Kitchen at
Holly—before

in addition to making your house more attractive, advertising a house with a brand new heater may very will net you more money than you spent on the upgrade.

Something else that you should keep in mind is the fact that your buyer wants to move in immediately. A house in "move-in condition" has a tremendous advantage over one that needs even a small bit of work. Buyers can finish the garage into a family room or change the paint in the living room if they don't like it, but they generally don't want to do it right away. They want to buy a house they can live in and live with right now. So be sure that you do not leave anything for the buyer to do immediately.

If you are male, you are already at a bit of a disadvantage in renovation because most married buyers are going to make decisions based on how the wife feels about the house. Having

Picture 29
Kitchen at
Holly—after

a female realtor or your wife giving you advice about colors and materials can be a huge help. You want to see the house through the buyer's eyes, not yours.

We still laugh about a bathroom that Jim painted in our first renovation. We had totally renovated the space, replacing everything including the wallboard, bathtub and tile. At the end of the renovation he chose a medium-blue paint and was quite proud of how it looked after he was finished painting. Except, it was just too masculine-looking for a primary bathroom that females would eventually use.

When our realtor visited one day she looked horrified and said emphatically, "Make it go away!" Three coats of beige paint later, the blue paint finally did go away. Jim is still bitter. But the eventual buyer is happy, and that's what counts.

The lesson we learned from Jim's Bold Blue Bathroom Escapade is that neutral colors are best. They might not be everyone's favorite, but a buyer will not feel the need to change the color right away.

This holds true for carpets, paint, tile, counter tops, cabinets and floors. You may have strong preferences for a certain "bold look," but trust us. Paint your *own* kitchen burgundy and peach with forest green trim. And paint your renovated house's kitchen off-white!

Another note on painting: There is no reason to be fancy. We save both time and money by asking our painter to paint everything the same color. Every room is a clean-looking eggshell color, and the walls are painted the same color as the ceilings. This enables your painter to spray rather than roll the paint on.

Your goal is to make the house look great, not fancy. As long as the buyer can move right in, he will be happy. He can repaint rooms in a certain color at his leisure as long as the current paint job is fresh and neutral in color.

Maximizing space can be very important, especially in smaller houses.

In one house we removed a wall oven (that had been illegally installed) and found ourselves looking at a large hole in a kitchen wall. Rather than simply put sheetrock over the hole, we enlarged the hole upwards a bit and installed two common wall cabinets, stacked and recessed, into the opening.

Picture 30
Good use of
space at Holly

Picture 31
Little things
can make a big
difference

The result was a lovely pantry that was a huge selling point in the otherwise small kitchen.

In that same house we gutted the main bathroom and found some dead space in a wall that was over a foot wide and deep in the wall opposite the vanity. We were able to transform this into an open closet for towels and toiletries.

Again, very little effort and expense, but a big pay-off. Basements may receive the same attention. We make sure that the walls and floors are painted, even in unfinished basements. The result is a space that looks inviting for use as storage or a workshop rather than a space that is not an asset.

Little things count. We pay attention to lighting and make sure that we install as many lights as we are able. And we are sure to use the maximum wattage allowed in all lighting fixtures. This makes the home look larger and brighter.

We always add track lighting over the sink in the kitchen. This makes it easy to throw light down on the counter top and on the sink area. Be sure to keep the lawn groomed, especially on weekends when realtors will be taking more people through the house.

More little things: Put a nice trash can and matching towels, cup and toothbrush holders in the bathrooms.

Be sure to add nice flowers in as many places as practical around the exterior. Use plug-in air fresheners to keep the house smelling nice. Make sure the windows and both the interior and exterior sills are clean. All doors should open and close properly.

Replace all of the interior door hardware so that it all matches and looks clean and shiny. You might even replace the interior door hinges with nice, new brass hinges if the old ones are old, rusted, or painted over. Add nice doormats. Replace the mailbox with a classy, fresh new one. The sum total expense for all of the things above is probably less than $200. But what a difference it will make!

Finally, have your wife, sister or mother go through the property and tell you what you may have done wrong or missed. Trust her judgment! She will inevitably see things that you did not, many of which can be cheaply and easily fixed.

If you follow these simple suggestions, you stand an excellent chance of making your house stand out from the crowd.

chapter **21**

Should I Allow Someone to Agree to Purchase the Property Before it is Fully Renovated?

CHAPTER 21   SHOULD I ALLOW SOMEONE TO AGREE TO PURCHASE THE PROPERTY BEFORE IT IS FULLY RENOVATED?

We have, on occasion, allowed neighbors and friends of neighbors to tour our renovation project as it is in process. This can help you by spreading the word around for potential buyers and by gaining good will in the neighborhood. One byproduct of this can be that you will have folks who want to buy the home before you are finished.

We started down this road once, and it seemed like a reasonable opportunity for both the buyer and us. The potential buyer wanted to save some money by purchasing the property and finishing it himself. And we were open to the idea of cashing out more quickly, as long as we could still turn a reasonable profit.

We did a market analysis and figured out a potential selling price if the house was finished, figured out what was left to do, how much more money we would have had to spend to finish, and how much of that savings we were willing to pass along to the buyer. This seemed reasonable enough.

But there were several problems. First, it is nearly impossible to figure out a value on an unfinished house. This is because the value is really set by the market, not by an appraisal. In other words, until the house is finished and on the market you really have no idea what it is worth. In this case, we eventually found that the value was tens of thousands of dollars greater than we were thinking it was while we were renovating. Had we sold it incomplete, we would have lost that money.

Another problem is that it is very difficult for a buyer to secure a mortgage on a property that he cannot inhabit. He must secure a construction loan, not a real mortgage. Additional problems are created by potential liability over the incomplete work. And all the time that you are negotiating this sale, you must suspend work so that you are not continuing to improve someone else's house!

Let's say you are aware of someone who wants to purchase the house and they would like you and your crew to do the final elements of the job to their own liking. Don't do it! You do not want to have the added confusion of having them take time selecting paint, fixtures and flooring. This will slow you down immensely. Indeed, this is why residential renovation in inhabited homes is so very expensive. The process moves slowly when the buyer is making decisions and changing his mind.

You will also find that pre-selling a home is far too risky when you learn how many contracts (with deposits) to purchase homes fall apart and are never brought to closing. We have experienced that about 20% to 30% of the homes we have had under contract have not gone to closing with the buyer. Imagine what would happen if you custom-finished a home for a buyer with floral wallpaper and orange carpet and then the deal fell through!

In short, we have found that the idea of selling an incomplete house, while appealing on paper, is a colossal headache and a bad business move.

How to Determine if You Want a Quick Sale or Not

CHAPTER 22 **HOW TO DETERMINE IF YOU WANT A QUICK SALE OR NOT**

You finished your renovation project! You are now ready to sell this thing and make loads of money. You need to decide at this point whether you want a quick sale or to try to fetch the highest price you can. There are few factors to consider.

Are home prices going up in your area? If so, you might want to be patient, set a high price and see what you can get for the home. You can learn a lot from your realtor about what homes are selling for in your neighborhood. Why not try listing the home 5% higher than the neighborhood comparables and see what happens?

A couple of years ago we had a property finished in June in an escalating market. We listed the house much higher than the neighborhood comparables and would you believe it? We sold the home for a price that was within a couple percent of our asking price! You never know who is out there that might fall in love with your property. So if market conditions are right, list it high and hope for a positive result.

Are prices flat or going down in your area? Sell that sucker quickly! There is no sense in paying interest on a property that is not appreciating in value. We sold two properties quickly by setting the price low because real estate values in our area at that time were flat. We are not real estate experts, but we do read the Wall Street Journal and other business publications and all signs indicate an overall flattening or even declining real estate market in the years to come.

Another area that will affect your decision for or against a quick sale is your financial position. Can you afford to keep paying interest on your loans if you decide to price your property high for a month or more? A 7% loan on $200,000 will be costing you more than $1,100 a month.

If your property is in a neighborhood where sale prices are relatively set in stone (+/- 3%) set the price at the average and sell it quickly. You may be lucky and have a bidding war!

A note about realtors. Realtors will want you to sell your property quickly. You will win them over to your way of thinking but know that they will want a quick sale. Here's why. It's simple math. If you list your property for $190,000 to sell it quick but could have listed it for $200,000 and sold it at that price with a little patience you have given up $10,000. Ten thousand dollars is a lot of money to you and me, but it is nothing to your realtor.

Your realtor is losing approximately $300, while you have lost $10,000. Realtors want you to list your property low because they will incur much lower costs in selling your home if it sells on its first weekend. There is nothing wrong with a realtor's bias toward working this way—you just need to know that this is how the dynamics work and set the price higher if you feel that that is the right thing to do.

chapter 23

How to Work With Realtors

Now that you have a relationship with a realtor, you must quickly learn their trade so that you can effectively work with them. Here are some basics.

Realtors work on commission, and that commission is generally paid by the seller. But a realtor does not earn 6% on the sale of your home. She must split that several ways. If a buyer's realtor is involved, 1% to 3% may go to the buyer's realtor or real estate company. And, of course, your realtor may work for a corporation and may need to share the profit with them. On your $250,000 house, the realtor is likely not making very much of the $15,000 sales commission.

The realtor's cut may go up if she can act as both the seller and buyer's realtor. That seems like a conflict of interest. That's because it is. There are disclosures that must be signed in that case, acknowledging that the realtor is working both sides of the transaction. And there are strict laws and accountability that act to ensure that the realtor does not take advantage of the situation lest she be stripped of her license. But it is still a conflict of interest. And it's the simple reality of the industry.

When you are the seller, it would seem that the realtor would want to help you to squeeze every last dollar out of your property so that they earn a greater commission. Wrong! Look at it this way: Your realtor wants to turn properties over quickly because it is in sheer volume that they can make the most money.

Let's say that you are trying to sell a property for $250,000 and you receive an offer of $230,000. And, in this case, you have agreed to pay your realtor a 4.5% sales commission. To you, that $230,000 offer is a loss of $29,100 off your asking price. To your realtor, it is a difference of $900. And this $900 would be split several ways.

Do you think that your realtor is going to be motivated to counsel you to hold out for your asking price when the reality is that she will only net $450 of the difference between your asking price and this offer? Hardly! She is looking at the likelihood of a quick sale if you accept the $230,000 offer and she can stop advertising and showing your house.

She is interested in volume, not an extra $450. So remember, even though you have a representative, you still control the deal. That's why you need to be familiar with as much of the real estate game as you can. If that $230,000 offer is truly reasonable, you should know that and not hold out for your asking price.

But if it is only a buyer looking for a steal, you should know that, too. This is where it really pays to have a good relationship with a trusted realtor whom you can challenge when you need to, but who will shoot straight with you when she knows best.

What if you have finished a renovation and your property does not sell immediately? One strategy is to drop price every two weeks. This keeps the property on the radar of the local realtors, since it represents a "new" opportunity each time you drop the price and keeps it on their radar. We know that this hurts… you were sure that you were going to get your asking price.

But remember, a product is worth only what someone is willing to pay for it, not what the experts say it is worth. And you want to move this property. It is costing you money to hold, and you have cash or credit tied up in it that is prohibiting you from moving on to other properties. All of this is a good reason to price your property reasonably at the start.

Another strategy that may pay off is to capitalize on the desire of the realtors working for buyers to make money. Rather than dropping the price, you might have your realtor make it known that you are prepared to "give back" an additional point or two in additional commissions to the buyer's realtor while keeping the sale price the same. This way the buyers' realtors will be much more motivated to show your home and encourage their clients to purchase it. At very least, this strategy is guaranteed to elicit some showings!

We advise that you keep in regular contact with your realtor while you are in buying or selling mode. They have other listings and other clients. You want to be just enough of a pest that they are motivated to give you their time and attention!

chapter **24**

How to Price Your House
Right for a Quick Sale

CHAPTER 24 **HOW TO PRICE YOUR HOUSE RIGHT FOR A QUICK SALE**

You have bought a great house at a great price and invested lots of time and money to finish the renovation, but you still have one important hurdle to clear. You must sell your house for a good price. Fortunately, the excellent realtor whom you chose several chapters ago will be a huge help. But you still must decide with your realtor how much you should ask for your newly renovated house. How do you decide?

First, have your realtor run a competitive market analysis and show you as many "comps" as possible. Comparing similar houses in the same neighborhood is the only way to determine an accurate estimation of local property values. Similar houses that have sold recently will show you what buyers are willing to pay.

It is likely that your house will be at or at least near the top of the range of similar homes which have sold, since yours will be newly renovated. (It is always surprising to us how many homes are put on the market in bad shape!) You have, in all likelihood, already done this exercise before you purchased the house. But now, several months later, you may find that there are better comps out there.

We have on several occasions found that the market changed significantly in the few short months that we were renovating the property. Hopefully, if the market has changed it will be in your favor! So now that you have an idea of what is reasonable to expect, you should set your price at a level that will guarantee a lot of interest from prospective buyers.Pricing your home at the absolute top of the market may only ensure that buyers will overlook your property. This is because of that old axiom: it's all about location. If a buyer can find a house that is in reasonable condition in a better neighborhood versus your perfect home in a less desirable neighborhood, guess which one he will usually pick? This is another reason why we resist over-improving a home, something we covered in an earlier chapter.

You should also have your realtor give you a quick tutorial on how realtors and buyers search the internet for homes. There are pricing levels that help them to classify houses, and you should be aware of these as you put your home on the market.

Never let your homes go over the "search barrier." In one of the towns we have worked, a 3 bedroom / 2 bath home goes for as high as $250,000. Even if your home is far better than others on the market we recommend that you set the price at $249,999. This is because of the way realtors will search the MLS for their clients. They will enter search parameters like (3 bedrooms, 2 baths, garage, basement, price range). The price range category will have round numbers ($200,000, $225,000, $250,000, etc.).

If realtors believe that the top end price for that neighborhood is $250,000, they may not enter a number larger than that as a search parameter. If you price your property at $255,000 you may have missed a large number of realtors who did not search that high. Your realtor will beat these and other truths into your head over time!

We watched this phenomenon happen to a friend recently. He priced his property at $205,000 and had very, very few people pay a visit. The house sat on the market for a long time until his realtor finally won the battle and convinced him to price the home at $199,000. It sold almost immediately.

In the end, your realtor is usually the best one to help you set an appropriate price for your property. Our realtor has grown with us and now knows how we work. In general we go with her recommendation. But she understands that we are willing to set a relatively high price and wait a little bit with most properties.

Remember our earlier advice on dealing with realtors; your realtor has little to gain by helping you to earn an extra $5,000 or $10,000. This is a lot of money to you, but her commission is a tiny fraction and she wants your house to sell quickly and be off her list. Be sure that your working relationship with your realtor is one characterized by clear and honest communication and you can expect good advice when it comes to pricing your house for sale.

chapter 25

How to Grow Your Business

Assuming that you are a novice and are starting small, there are three distinct stages that your renovation business may go through.

- **Stage 1**—You do most of the work, but you hire contractors for big or technical jobs.

- **Stage 2**—You function as a General Contractor and hire contractors to do most or all of the work.

- **Stage 3**—You hire a General Contractor to do the entire project on your behalf.

We started in Stage 1 and lingered there for several years. There were several reasons for that. First, in the early years we didn't know much about working with contractors. And frankly, we enjoyed (and still enjoy) the hands-on work. And there was something very satisfying about coming home dirty, and it was gratifying to see the fruit of our own labor.

And there was one other thing…. we made more money that way! Every dollar we might have spent on a laborer or contractor was money that we could "pay ourselves." But it only took a few projects to cure us of that view. What we found was that renovating a home is a lot of work! Satisfying and gratifying, yes. But a lot of work! And we began to figure out that if we paid some folks who could do "grunt work" (demolition, cleaning up, filling dumpsters, etc) for a small wage, we would have more time on our hands for other things that counted for more.

We also figured out that there were some jobs that would take us twice or three times as long as a professional would take, and the pros would do an even better job than we could in less time than we would have spent. So we began to seriously consider the real cost of our time and concluded that there was much wisdom in moving to Stage 2 as quickly as possible.

Do you ever wonder how people can make money selling inexpensive products like a 50 cent pack of gum? The answer is obvious. Volume! And although you may make less money on a particular project if you move to Stage 2, you can make it up in volume. As a General Contractor instead of a laborer, you have the ability to manage more than one project at a time.

When we were immersed in our early renovation projects, we barely had time for anything else even when we were only working on one house. But if you are supervising contractors to do work for you, you can have several projects at once and increase your potential profit dramatically. Volume!

In Stage 3, you become something of an investor, not a renovator. You employ others to make the majority of decisions and to do all of the real work. We are not there yet... and we're not sure we really want to be there anytime soon. There is obviously a lot of money to be made when you turn that corner and you won't be coming home sweaty and dirty!

Sore Backs, Sore Heads and Sore Butts

We think that these three phrases can portray each of the three stages you will move through in this business. In each stage, a different kind of effort is required. Here is a quick look at each, and why you might or might not wish to grow your business into the next stage.

In Stage 1, which we will characterize the "sore back stage," you will be doing the majority of the work yourself. This will require that you either know how to do a variety of the renovation jobs you are faced with, can learn quickly, or have a talented brother in law with a willing spirit. You had better love getting your hands dirty, because you will be doing everything from demolishing walls, to clearing brush, to laying vinyl flooring.

It will obviously take you a lot of time to get your renovation done if you are a one man or even a two man band and your renovation could drag on for many months if the amount of work that needs to be done is extensive. If you are not accomplished at some particular trade, you run the risk of leaving your home with shoddy or even unsafe work.

Given the list of negative implications enumerated above, why would you want to consider being a Stage 1 business? There are several reasons.

First, your risk in Stage 1 is low. This is certainly not to say that there is no risk, but it is much less than in Stages 2 and 3. You will almost certainly only be working on one home at a time. If the market flattens, interest rates rise, you become disabled, the cost of materials spiral or there is any other unforeseen circumstance, your total risk is limited to one property and the money you have invested in it.

You may also like Stage 1 if you want to start slowly and learn the building and real estate trades. There is no substitute for solid, hands-on experience. Even after your first flip, you will be amazed when you think about all you have learned. You may also really enjoy working with your hands. For us, demolishing a wall or renovating a bathroom is a welcome change from our full-time jobs and one that we look forward to with great enthusiasm.

There are few things more satisfying to us than doing a task that has a beginning and an end—a dynamic that is in short supply in our regular jobs! Since we are in a partnership, we also work together most of the time and really enjoy one another's company. If you find it difficult to locate contractors or if you have difficulty negotiating with or supervising others, you will not be working with a lot of people in Stage 1, which would be an advantage for you.

And if your financing is limited or if your earning goals are modest, Stage 1 also makes the most sense. As you can see, there are more than a few reasons why you might never desire to grow your business any farther than this. If flipping a property every 9 months to a year is enough for you, why mess with success?

Moving from Stage 1 to Stage 2 requires some experience and business sense. This is why we have characterized **Stage 2** as the

"sore head" stage. In Stage 2 you need to find more people to help you, trust more people, and supervise more people.

Relationships are wonderful, but they are also occasionally messy! If you engage an incompetent contractor, one who will not complete work on time, or one who makes your life difficult in any way, you will quickly reminisce about how uncomplicated your life was in Stage 1.

In Stage 2 your profit margin will shrink dramatically, because you will be paying people to do work that you could have done "for free" (other than the real, but hidden cost of your valuable time and sweat). You will essentially become the General Contractor for the renovation of the homes you will purchase and will be employing contractors to do the majority of the work on every project.

If you do enjoy some of the hands-on work you may certainly reserve some of that for yourself to do, but most of the job will be completed by professionals. You will be risking much more money because you will owe more money to more people, people who will expect to be paid on time regardless of what difficulties you incur personally or professionally.

Stage 2 will require several things that you did not need in Stage 1. First, you will need a larger and quicker source of funds. Your outlay will be greater, in that you will be paying laborers and other workers who are doing tasks that you yourself did in Stage 1. Therefore, you will need more money, and you will need access to it more quickly.

You will now also have the potential of fielding several renovations at the same time, so your potential outlay could be several times greater than in Stage 1. You will also need a larger pool of reliable and trustworthy contractors and laborers. As you move through Stage 1, keep your eyes open for people who might do even more work for you in the future!

The key to your success will largely hinge on your ability to find folks who will work for you quickly, with excellence, and for a reasonable wage. This is where you will be glad that you bought that cold drink for a contractor or offered a friendly word to a laborer back in Stage 1!

Although there are inherent difficulties in Stage 2, there are also many advantages. Assuming that you desire to and are able to work effectively with contractors, you will be able to field two, three or even five projects simultaneously with roughly the same amount of effort as in Stage 1. This effort will be of a different kind—it will largely be relational and organizational energy that you are expensing rather than physical exertion. And although your profit margin per project will shrink, your total earning potential will grow through volume.

If you are not skilled at the hands-on aspects of a renovation, if you really enjoy meeting and working with people and if your earning goals are higher, you may wish to make the move to Stage 2 as quickly as is practical in your situation.

We characterize **Stage 3** as the **"sore butt"** stage. In Stage 3 you are a manager, pure and simple. You may never see the inside of many of the houses that you will buy. You will employ a General Contractor, perhaps even full-time, to manage your projects. Your work environment will be largely confined to a desk, a computer and a cell phone. And you will not be doing home renovation part-time.

To be candid, we are not in Stage 3 yet, and we are not at all sure that we ever wish to be. We had a tough time giving up the work we enjoy doing to make the jump to Stage 2! In fact, we often reserve one fairly significant aspect of the renovation to do ourselves—a kitchen or a bathroom or two - just because we love to do it.

In Stage 3, you take on an enormous amount of risk. You may be fielding dozens of projects simultaneously and will be obligated to dozens, if not hundreds, of employees and contractors. Your profit

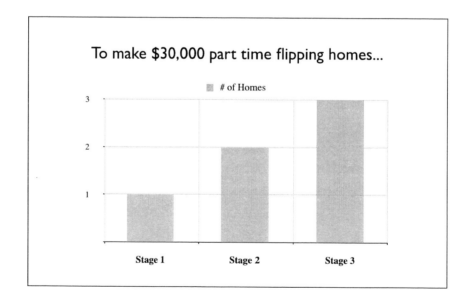

margin per house will shrink to a fraction of what it was in Stage 1. But your earning potential will be virtually unlimited. Resources for making this transition abound, but we will not endeavor to speak to that transition at all. If you turn that corner, be sure to let us know. Perhaps we'll buy *your* book!

As you can see from the above chart it is our experience that in order for a part-timer to make $30,000 a year doing this business they will have to do more or less homes per year depending on which stage they are in.

The highest profit/home is in stage 1 which makes sense since you are doing most of the work yourself. We have found that in Stage 2 we have made a profit of about half we did in stage 1. Now notice how the line begins to take a less extreme decline from stage 2 to stage 3. We believe that Stage 3 flattens out and can actually

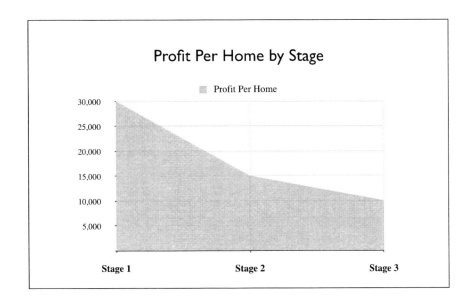

increase with a higher volume of houses flipped due to economies of scale.

In Stage 3 you will be dealing with what major corporations deal with on a daily basis. The more efficiency you get out of your people and partners the better the profit per unit will be. If you intend on growing into Stage 3 it would make good sense to prepare yourself to think like big business. Once you arrive at Stage 3 it may be time to quit your job and start increasing the number of homes you buy as it simply becomes a numbers game at this point. 10 homes equals $100,000-$125,000, 30 homes becomes $300,000-$400,000.

Keep in mind that with all of the graphs above are based on our experience in this as a part-time endeavor. If you do this full time your results could be significantly different.

It takes some time, experience and planning to make the jump to Stage 2. But we never promised that you would get rich quickly. Our advice would be to be careful and really think through the implications of moving to the next stage. If this is merely a fun and lucrative hobby, as it was for us in the beginning, Stage 1 can be a great place to be. But if you are serious about doing more of this and find yourself developing a real "knack" for this kind of thing, moving to the next stage may be a promising idea indeed.

If you are contemplating moving to Stage 2, there would be some questions you should ask yourself. First, was your track record good in Stage 1? Were you able to generate a decent profit? Did you effectively identify and work with a variety of contractors?

Were you able to study market conditions and buy and sell your houses quickly and painlessly? Have you assembled a capable team; a great realtor, a cadre of contractors; a capable CPA and adequate financiers? Is your family supportive of this move? Does there continue to be a decent market for buying and selling in your area? If the answers to these questions are affirmative, this could be a good move for you. If you are not sure about a few of them, you might do well to gain more experience and resources.

We believe that you can make this jump by "buying your way in" or by "earning your way in." What we mean by this is that you can simply commit a large amount of time and capital to make up for your lack of natural ability and relational assets, or you can build your business on the strength of your experience and relationships. I'd bet you know which one we advocate!

Did you know that over 75% of start-up businesses in the U.S. fail before one year is over, and before five years are out, 95% have failed? Although we are not experts on the survival of small businesses, we would bet that there is a strong correlation between the failure of those that "bought" their start and those that eventually failed. There simply is no substitute for experience and relationships. If you really know how to do a job and you have others around you who want to see you do well, you have a strong chance of success.

You might do well to test the water as you plan your jump to Stage 2. Ask your family, friends, and others who are aware of your renovation business what they think of the idea. Encourage them to be honest with you and not to tell you what they think you want to hear. Then ask some of your contractors what they think. Would they be willing to work with you on a consistent basis? Do they believe in your ability to run a renovation business? The feedback you will receive will be very helpful for you as you make your decision.

One last piece of free advice: be sure that this is something that you like to do. It is a personal value of ours that the desire to make money is a very bad motivation for doing anything. This world is full of miserable rich people. When asked how much money was enough money, John D. Rockefeller said, "Just a little bit more."

If this is a business that brings you joy and satisfaction along with a financial reward, that is terrific. But we didn't set out to become rich. We set out to meet a challenge, the challenge of starting an enjoyable enterprise. And we hoped that along with meeting that challenge we would earn money that we could use to benefit our families, friends, and some charitable works that are important to us.

chapter 26

Take Your Time and Build Relationships With Key People

As we have stated several times before, relationships are the things that will move you forward in this business. If you cannot or will not work effectively with people, do not expect to be successful over the long haul in business or in life. You will be surprised how many people you will come in contact with as you renovate homes, and you will be surprised how many of them can help you in significant ways if you are willing to invest a bit in building relationships with them.

We have mentioned at other points in this book the importance of having good relationships with contractors. They have the ability to do work more quickly, more cheaply and with more attention to detail if they are motivated to do so. And money is not the only or the most effective motivator. Working for people who appreciate us is very often a stronger motivator than money. And we have found this to be true when dealing with contractors. If a contractor sees your relationship as a potential long-term association which will be a win-win, they will be glad to help you to get where you want to go.

So we have found it useful to communicate right from the start that we would like to see the particular job we are hiring them to do as the first of many opportunities. We have also referred our better contractors to others, being sure that the contractor knows where the referral came from. Let's face it, you need all the help you can get, and contractors can be extremely helpful to you over time.

The same principles may apply to your relationships with other key people. Take building inspectors as a great example. These people hold a tremendous amount of power over your success or failure. You can imagine what a nightmare it would be to face a nit-picky inspector who will not take your word for granted and who holds you to the letter of the building code. They can cost you immeasurable time and money as you remedy a seemingly infinite list of deficiencies. On the other hand, picture a friendly inspector who trusts that you have done a good job, and who will give you the benefit of the doubt. Sometimes the difference between the two is only the difference in how they are treated.

We try to make sure that we are present anytime an inspector calls. We go out of our way to be friendly, engaging, and humorous. Inspectors have a difficult job and bear lots of responsibility. Their job is easier if they feel that they can trust you, so we try to do everything we can to earn their trust. This may mean "turning ourselves in" when it comes to small and easily fixed items. For instance, in a final inspection one inspector pointed out an exterior electrical outlet that was not ground-fault protected.

We instantly told him that we had two other such outlets that he had missed, and assured him that we would fix all three of them within an hour. We might also ask questions that represent a certain amount of overkill to demonstrate our good faith. We might install an extra carbon monoxide detector in the basement (which is not necessary in most states) and make a point of asking if we have sufficiently protected the home.

What we are trying to communicate is that we are willing to submit to his or her judgment and that we have not tried to cut corners. We have found that with some relational grease, the gears can be lubricated sufficiently to create a real advantage for us. We have been given extra latitude by inspectors on several renovations because the inspectors were convinced that we did quality work and would deal with any oversights quickly and responsibly. So be sure to come across as friendly, cooperative and competent.

We have also worked hard to build relationships with the principle employees of lending institutions. Whenever we visit the bank we are friendly and engaging. In one case we were given a check as a loan from an individual only three days before we needed the money to purchase a property.

Upon arrival at the bank to pick up a check for closing, we were horrified to find that the loan proceeds had not cleared because the check was drawn on an investment account and the funds needed to be verified, a process that can easily take five business days. In any other case we may have been out of luck.

But the head bank teller moved heaven and earth to make exceptions and give us access to the money simply because she wanted to help us. And why did she want to help us? Because she liked us. And she liked us because we had been friendly in the past and had built a good rapport with her. Relationships can grease the wheels on loans, get you refunds for bounced check fees, and gain you many other advantages that you may need from time to time. Besides, treating people well is just the right thing to do.

chapter 27

Staying Organized Through the Process

If you are starting a business, you will need to be organized. This should go without saying. The only way you will be able to know whether or not your business has been successful in the end is if you are organized enough to make a good evaluation of what you have spent and what you have made. You also need to be organized enough to keep track of bills that are coming due, taxes that will need to be paid, etc. Being well organized is not negotiable. If you are not gifted in this area, you need to find someone who is and enlist their help.

When we have had only one property under renovation at a time, being organized has been fairly simple. Nearly every expense is related to that project, so that simplifies things. Every check and every deposit made to or from our checking account would be related to one project. But even then, it is useful to have a system that enables you to figure out exactly what aspect of the project you are spending money on. As you gain experience, you will want to begin to build a knowledge base that tells you what things really cost.

We have often been shocked to find out how far off our original estimates we have been on some aspects of the renovation. And usually those categories where we have been far off are ones where we spend a few dollars at a time, not categories where we have employed contractors to do large jobs. Being organized enough to track expenses within categories can give you a real advantage when it comes time to estimate the renovation cost of your second, third and tenth houses!

So how do you do it? You don't have to be an accountant! Any simple off-the-shelf accounting software like Quicken or Quick Books can be a real help. Using Quicken we have simply created an account for each property we are working on as sub-accounts of our checking account.

Any expense or deposit related to a particular renovation is keyed in to that account, and, in the end, we have an accurate picture of our net gain or loss. A somewhat more complicated, but more effective, approach would be to create sub-categories for each of these project accounts, and this way you can track expense categories like "bathroom," "kitchen," "landscape" etc. At the conclusion of the project be sure to take some time to generate reports that will inform the estimates on your next renovation.

It is also critical that you keep receipts. Which receipt? EVERY receipt! Your accountant will bless you, and the IRS will be impressed if you are audited. Remember, every expense is deducted from your taxable income, so your friendly IRS agent may really want to see the back-up for the expenses you are claiming. It would be wise to keep these in some filing system more sophisticated than a manila envelope, although we must confess that we do have more than a few of those big, brown envelopes crammed with Home Depot receipts.

chapter **28**

Incorporating and
Accounting

It is tempting to start renovating homes without becoming incorporated. When we started out we were not incorporated because we were just "experimenting" with this business. We thought that if we wanted to continue with the business we would become incorporated *then*. Looking back we were stupid. Yes, stupid. We should have incorporated. For less than $500 dollars you can become incorporated yourself—do it. Here is why.

Even though you may be doing a modest business, if there would ever be legal action taken against you, you need to keep your personal assets separate from your renovation activity. Laws vary in various states, but in New Jersey we believe that forming a "limited liability corporation" is the best choice. LLCs in New Jersey offer you slightly better tax advantages than S corporations. This enables you to have a partner, and keep all of your personal assets far apart from any activity related to your business. People can and do sue for anything these days. If you are not incorporated you become a much more attractive target. Attorneys and their clients are more likely to sue (and sue for larger amounts) if you have more money or assets to pay them. If your personal assets are up for grabs, you are a target.

Another wise idea is to hire an accountant. While your business is modest in scale, you will find that the services of a local accountant can be quite reasonably priced. Your accountant will help you to know how to keep records, file the proper tax information, and can even help you with the incorporation process.

Finding a good accountant will also protect you when the IRS comes looking around your business. Face it—most businesses will be audited at some point. When you, a non-CPA, do your taxes, you are on the hook if something is wrong. Even if it was a simple, ignorant error. Adding an accountant to the mix puts them somewhat on the hook if you are ever audited. They have a vested interest in making sure that your taxes are correct.

Having an accountant also helps keep you honest. Your accountant will tell you what is legal and what is illegal as far as accounting goes. There are significant tax advantages to those who know the ins and outs of tax law. When you have an accountant you can simply give them all the information they ask for and relax. And in the rare cases where they get you into trouble, you have every right to sue them.

In the end, having an accountant do your taxes for the business makes great sense. Don't you think the countless hours you spend trying to file returns could be spent better elsewhere? A few hundred dollars for an accountant is chump change—do it.

chapter **29**

You're On Your Way!

Congratulations! You have finished reading our book. You are now on your way to an exciting and enjoyable career in home renovation. Even if you never quit your day job, you stand an excellent chance of being successful in this business if you are patient and prudent. Build your business slowly and carefully and have fun doing it! We never set out to get rich. We set out to see if we could excel at something that we enjoyed, while exploring our own gifts and talents. If your focus is similar, you will do well.

We hope that as your business develops, so will your skills. Remember the checklist of things you needed back in chapter 3? Many of those were skills and character qualities. It will be fun for you to watch as your own portfolio of skills and abilities grows. And remember, people skills are the key! There is simply no shortcut for relationships, and relationships will be mutually beneficial nearly every time. Work hard in this area and you will find that you will enjoy yourself more and your business will be more successful.

As you get a house or two under your belt, be sure to let us know how it's going! We would enjoy the feedback. You may find a variety of helpful resources through our website at www.realisticflipping.com. On the website's forum you may also give us your feedback on how useful our book may have been to you. We look forward to hearing from you.

Good luck! And have fun!

The Checklist—
Putting Things in Order

It is difficult for us to give you an absolutely step-by-step order
for your renovation project, but the process is somewhat linear.
With the caveat that you will necessarily need to double back from
time to time, and understanding the fact that we cannot account
for things that go badly or totally wrong, let us attempt to set out a
sample renovation project from start to finish. Nearly all of these
steps are discussed more fully elsewhere in this book, but for
the sake of putting them in order, here they are with a very short
discussion of each.

1) Assess your resources. We addressed this idea in detail in earlier
chapters. But do not shortcut this step. You really do need to decide
whether or not the renovation game is a good match for your
personal and corporate resources. Remember to consider not only
your skills and the availability of financing, but the "soft costs"
you will incur. These include the inevitable strain on your family,
time away from your full-time occupation, and the loss of vacation
and free time.

2) Develop your team. First, you need a realtor. You will obviously
need help buying a home to renovate. You will also need help
selling it once you are done. Be sure to employ a realtor who you
can work well with and who understands exactly what you are
trying to do. Do you have an accountant? A partner? People from
whom you can get good advice? A reliable home inspector who
knows what you are trying to do?

3) Get organized. If you have a partner, who will handle each
aspect of the project? Who will pay bills, keep receipts and engage

contractors? Do you have the filing system and software that you need to stay organized?

4) Assess market conditions. Is this the right time and place to begin this business, or a specific project? Will you renovate to sell or to rent? How does the current market impact your project? Is it rising or in decline?

5) Secure financing. It is imperative that you know how you will pay for your initial purchase and all of the renovations and holding costs before you even begin to look at properties. The amount of money that you can come up with will have a bearing on the kind of market you will search.

6) Decide where to look for homes and begin the search process. After you have targeted an area, you and your realtor will begin looking for homes in earnest.

7) Estimate your total costs for a particular property and then make your offer. If you were not able to have your home inspector give you a quick report prior to making an offer, be sure to make receipt of that report the one contingency on the sale. This will protect you from any catastrophic issue uncovered by the inspector. If your offer is accepted, congratulations! You will soon be a homeowner. But hopefully not for very long!

8) Prior to closing on your property, begin the process of scheduling contractors. You may not have full, or even any, access to the property before closing. But hopefully in the process of inspecting it you have figured out which jobs you are going to sub-

contract. Get those folks lined up as close to your closing date as possible! Having a hauling company get a dumpster to the property on closing day will be your first priority in most cases.

9) Endorse a really big check over to the title company. You now own a home.

10) Walk through the house over several hours, carefully taking notes. You will have absolutely missed a lot of things in your initial inspection. Compile a list of jobs, materials, and contractors needed. You can also begin to make notes on the eventual layout of the kitchen and bathrooms if you are doing extensive renovation on these. If you find odd sized spaces, you might even need to custom order cabinets, countertops, etc.

11) If there is any possibility of saving the floor surfaces (carpets or hardwood floors), be sure to get a bunch of cardboard, tape it down with making tape (not duct tape that leaves a residue!), and then cover all of that with heavy plastic sheeting, taped down as well. You will have more potentially destructive traffic than you can imagine, and you will save yourself a lot of money and trouble if you don't damage the floors. Even if you plan to refinish the hardwood floors, be sure to protect them from scratches and ground-in dirt at the start.

12) Demolition and clean-up will be your first priority. If you can do all of this in a day or two and be done with the majority of it, you'll be glad later. Doubtless there will be leftover trash, yard waste and the refuse from removing walls, old cabinets, countertops, toilets and vanities, etc. to throw in your dumpster.

(We suggest leaving that old refrigerator and one toilet for a while. You can deal with them later, and it's nice to have their use while you're working!)

13) If you are planning to lay down grass seed at some point, doing this very early in the project is a good idea. In fact, doing much of the landscaping early on is a nice idea because it makes the house more attractive right from the start. If you get some interest in the neighborhood, you may have an easier time selling the house later.

14) If you need a new roof, do that or have it done at the start. You do not want any leaks to destroy your new renovation! The same goes for resolving drainage issues outside. You will want to stop any potential damage right away and give all soil and wood surfaces the maximum time to dry out.

15) Exterior doors and window replacement, if necessary, should be done near the start of the job.

16) Plumbing and electrical issues may be dealt with next. These may involve cutting into walls, drilling holes, etc., so get these done early. Your contractors will appreciate it if you do not present them with finished walls to work around!

17) If you are having a heating system replaced, it may take a while to get your contractor scheduled. You should probably put this towards the front end of the project. If there needs to be ductwork done or holes cut in the interior walls for return vents, you need to do that early.

18) Are you adding insulation to the attic? Doing this early will save you heat in the winter and make it cooler while you work in the summer.

19) Interior renovation of walls, bathrooms and kitchen can all begin next. There is no magic as to the order, but do not install appliances, vanities, cabinets or new lighting fixtures until you have your painter come through. He will be grateful that he does not have to tape things, and the job will look more professional if everything has paint behind it.

20) If you are replacing interior doors and trim, be sure that these are done before your painter comes. If you are not replacing the doors, but only painting them, leave the old hinges on and then replace them after the painter has left. This will save him time and make it look better in the end. Door handles and strikers should be removed before the painter comes, and then replaced with fresh hardware after he leaves.

21) Floors are last. Install carpet and refinish hardwood floors.

22) Before you have actually finished the house, get it under a listing contract with your realtor! You will want to have her schedule a realtors' walk-through a day or two before it actually hits the market. You can have the FOR SALE sign up a week early, too. You want this house to hit MLS the minute you are done!

23) Finishing touches! Add matching towels, soap dish and trashcan in the bathrooms. Welcome mat out front. Fresh potted

flowers on the front porch. Anything you can do to make the house look warm and inviting.

24) Field offers on your house. Get it sold! And start looking for another project!

25) Do your final accounting. Be sure that all receipts are properly filed, bills are paid, and your accountant is satisfied with your record keeping before you get too far removed from this project.